A Secular Gospel

More Essays for Freethinkers

Chris Highland

© 2021 Chris Highland
Cover photograph by Chris Highland
Friendly Freethinker (www.chighland.com)

"[This strange experience] seems supernatural, but only because it is not understood. Anyhow, it seems silly to make so much of it, while the natural and common is more truly marvelous and mysterious than the so-called supernatural. Indeed most of the miracles we hear of are infinitely less wonderful than the commonest of natural phenomena, when fairly seen."

The Gospel of John Muir

(*My First Summer in the Sierra*, 1911)

CONTENTS

Introduction
1 Should We Fear or Cheer the Rise of Secularism?
2 Truth in a Post-Truth World
3 Turtles, Snakes, Rabbits and the Human Race
4 Learning the Language of Humanity
5 Still Points of History Along an Appalachian River
6 In the Galaxy of Religion, Resistance is Not Futile
7 Who Holds the Keys to the Kingdom, or Safe Sanctuaries?
8 Wonder is Wonder, Breathing is Breathing
9 Shakers, Trappists, and the Inclusive Dance of Simplicity
10 Thomas Merton, Shakers and the Paradise Myth
11 Symbols and Statues of Liberty and Responsibility
12 Is it True All Religions Worship the Same God?
13 How Do We Know What an Atheist Believes?
14 Suffering, Stuffering and Stumbling through Sickness
15 Yoruba: the Greatest Religion You've Never Heard Of
16 Jesus, John Wayne and Militant Masculinity
17 Journey to the Forest of Freethought: A Secular Parable
18 The Pleasure of Discovering You Are Wrong
19 The New American Religion of Nature
20 Freethought, Faith and the Future
21 Tom Paine's Church
22 When Science Becomes "Spirituality"

23 Walls of Mirrors, Windows or Sliding Doors
24 Sacrament of a Secular Saint
25 Heaven, Hope and Humanism
26 Secular in the Sanctuary
27 The Day I Went to Hell
28 Memorials (and Weddings) Without God
29 Farkhunda: Martyr for Us All
30 The Bible of Nature (Secular Scripture)
31 Last Supper for the Dying Church
32 Damn My Secular Soul
33 The New Secular

Afterword: Streaming, and, The Silent Skipping Stone

About the Author

INTRODUCTION

Standing in late afternoon sunshine, filling my lungs with fresh Appalachian air, I watched as our typical mountain summer weather drama was beginning. Bathed in a hot and humid stillness under a bright blue sky, suddenly in the distance, a deep rumble and boom ... an approaching thunderstorm. As the clouds rolled in and darkened, the scent of rain wafted through the trees, sending a chill over me. The dark black, gray and white clouds began their regular battle against the cerulean backdrop above. The show grew louder until I felt irresistibly drawn into the play. Thunderclaps echoed around the valley, then crashed overhead, punctuated with bright flashes and heavier raindrops. Immersed in the full sensual moment, I became a participant in this thrilling natural episode on the sky-screen. Out of the sound and silence, words emerged, then a poem formed in my head. Later, I posted my rumbling reflections on "Friendly Freethinker":

Cloud cannons roll
Beyond, nearer
Sky skirmishes engage
Armies in the air
Civil War in the up yonder
Gray against the Blue
Sunrays cut by swords of light
Billowing bursts of White
To hold or free the Black

What did people in 1863 hear
here in these mountain hollers?
Did they wonder:
Storm
or
Seige?
Rain
or
Ruin?
As the sky was torn
so the people.

The backstory is that I had been re-reading Wilma Dykeman's famous book, *The French Broad*, on the river and the region here in Western North Carolina. Her telling of the history in these mountains includes the storm of the Civil War, the secessionist storm that tore families, communities and country apart. Dykeman lived just up the street from our house, deeper in the "holler." The same stream that flows by the small house where she penned pages of *The French Broad* bubbles across the land where I now live, and babbles down into the French Broad itself. Describing the aftermath of that bloody conflict of the 1860's, she wrote: *"As soon as the first soldier turned home toward the mountains and left war behind him, so soon began another cycle in human renewal in this part of the South. The pieces were smashed, the pattern was lost, but the processes of life were as sure as time, sure as the river."*

Such beautiful writing. How to paint a picture on the canvas of the Blue Ridge when so much of the paint is blood and the frame so broken? Yet, this is the task, chosen much for your thoughts on my continuing questions. All us readers say Thank You to the chaplain of the bits & bytes & printing press. Gratitude." She respects my background in chaplaincy and my urge to keep writing and publishing musings and meditations. Another reader, emerging from evangelical life, wrote to me after reading *Broken Bridges*: "I have been looking for books and other resources to help me discover ways to enter this new step in my life. This great book offered a perspective into relating to people of other faiths/no faiths that finally made sense to me ... it gave me the hope that I can build bridges and love people simply because we are human."

I couldn't ask for a more encouraging response to my writings. Like the classes I teach on Freethought, my books, columns, essays, blogposts, poems, all are grounded, centered, rooted in the greater good. At least that's my intention. I'm not a bomb-thrower or bridge-burner, though I think I have a good sense of when something needs to be dismantled or naturally disintegrate. My intrinsic humanism (not always aligned with "official" Humanism) leads me to focus attention on the positive, constructive, helpful ways to invite us into conversation, perhaps even collaboration—hell, just learning to live in the same neighborhoods without fighting.

In Dykeman's story of the river, one river passing through time and turmoil, those who survive on the land, nourished by the streams, find a way to return, to come back in tattered uniforms, Gray or Blue. Though much of that disheartening division continues in our day, we are left with the same thing left to them: the rivers, mountains, forests, wildlife, and the challenge of how to be human, and how to live in human community.

or forced upon those who know, or sense they know, this world is all we have—a strange mix of wonder and war, hubris and humility, ruin and rebuilding, and repainting ... after the storms.

So, my poem reflects the inescapable battle with ourselves mirrored in the elements, the weather, climate, Nature itself. We can't seem to stop projecting ourselves out there, up there, in our ceaseless anthropomorphic dance. Surely the poem is not literal, and yet, perhaps in some atmospheric way, I was a participant in the drama, and the play and stage and other actors were not human—but like me, fully, completely, naturally secular.

This is the heart of secularism, humanism, naturalism, freethought. For me, it's all of these and more, because the "heart" *is* the "head" and to be human and tell the human story is to be consistently conscious of being a true participant, even when observing the drama on small and grand stages. We are the audience on stage, and truth is, Nature is not acting, not pretending—this is non-fiction, and so are we.

The essays in this book are primarily drawn from my weekly "Highland Views" columns published in the *Asheville Citizen-Times*, supplemented with a selection of blogposts. I see myself as an actor in each chapter, writing the script as I live it, drawing on my observations of the world near and far. I see or read something and hear a distant boom, a bass note rumbles in my mind's holler and I know I have to think about it, write about it—is it a storm or siege? Brainstorms are real and regular.

After reading my book, *Was Jesus a Humanist?: and other questionable essays*, a woman commented: "Thanks so

If anything can be called "gospel" anymore, it has to be centered here, on Earth, the earth, flowing with the rivers, swirling with the currents of common sense, critical thinking and finding our own way home together, back to what really matters—what is that for you?

Chris Highland

Asheville, North Carolina

Fall 2021

To
Critical Thinkers
and the
Consciously Compassionate

1

Should We Fear or Cheer the Rise of Secularism?

Definitions of the term "secular" come from Latin, "saeculum": the present age. Emphasis is on "attitudes and activities that have no religious basis." In Astronomy, it refers to "slow changes in the motion of the sun or planets."

Given these meanings, it never ceases to amaze me that so many fear secular ideas and secular people. Talk about "slow changes." Personally, I think we should celebrate the word, since it isn't anti-religious but offers a basis for any chosen worldview or belief, and protects everyone because it's not beholden to any particular faith.

A famous preacher claims it has "infiltrated" the nation and "stormed through the gates" of America. In his mind, it's a "very dangerous" threat to people of faith and our whole way of life.

The boogeyman? Secularism. And the scariest part of it, apparently, is that it's "godless." However, another definition of secularism doesn't emphasize that. It is "the principle of separation of the state from religious institutions." Secularism guards against theocracy.

Does any of this sound familiar? We need only think back to the 1950's. People were so scared of "the menace" of Communism and its atheism (though not all Communists are atheists) that people were tried in the court of public opinion and our godly protectors added "under God" to the Pledge. That was supposed to expose the non-religious who would choose not to say those words.

Seems to me, when we judge, exclude or divide people based on religious beliefs, we actually threaten our own freedom to follow our conscience.

God-less doesn't mean Good-less. When we define people by what they don't have—home-less, job-less, god-less—it seems that it makes us all "less": less united, less free, less human. There's an assumption a person without religious faith is less of a good citizen, maybe less ethical.

Does Secularism worry you? Fact is, any "ism" needs to be scrutinized. A philosophy or worldview (including religious "ism") is open to question and investigation. Secularism sees this world as the only one we can experience—the only one we know anything about—one planet to share. We know nothing about any other world. Many religious people, whose faith is "grounded" in another world, hear that as a threat—an imagined secular attack.

Nearly one quarter of Americans consider themselves "religiously unaffiliated" (PRRI.org). That doesn't mean they are secular; they just don't identify as religious.

Secularists (including humanists, freethinkers, agnostics and many atheists) are not seeking to destroy faith or remove all religion from society. Some believers want to "bring (their) God back" into schools and government, but many other believers join the secular community in resisting that. Most humbly considerate people of faith aren't concerned with forcing their faith on others—they're too busy addressing the needs of this world (perhaps using Jesus as their model) to be distracted by another world.

I've spoken with a few evangelicals whose faith isn't so much about the after-life but the before-death. That doesn't make them converts to secularism, just sensible.

In my days of youthful evangelicalism, a friend took me to the home of a Mormon family. I was uncomfortable and they could tell. The mother sat down by me and asked what was bothering me. "I think the Devil has deceived Mormons and your faith is not of God." I could see she was genuinely hurt, and to this day I feel a pang of embarrassment that I said that. We were steeped in a culture "under siege" by the forces of Evil, feeling our own satanic panic. Someone was out to get us, to attack our faith and take our God away. Now I wonder: was our faith so weak? Was our God so small?

If there was some force, power, philosophy or political ideology seeking to rid the world of great literature, art or ideas, I would stand beside anyone to resist. If someone made it their mission to tell people they couldn't pray, read their holy book or practice their faith, I would stand up and speak out. But I don't see or hear that.

The preachers of paranoia, who fill masses of minds with fear-based faith, are the ones to stand against. This is one powerful way believers and nonbelievers can stand together in resistance. A good secular thing to do!

"Secularism" is not "infiltrating" our communities to take anyone's faith or freedom away. There is no devilish monster sneaking around to make us all atheists (or even seculars).

Are there people who would like us to believe the same things, giving up freedom of choice and rational freethinking to fearfully follow their "authorities"? Sure. Chances are they're not secular.

2

Truth in a Post-Truth World

On her engaging podcast, "The Last Archive," historian Jill Lepore draws listeners to ask: "Who killed Truth?," leading us to wonder about "The Rise of Doubt." The program is described as "a show about how we know what we know and why it seems, lately, as if we don't know anything at all." Lepore keeps it entertaining as she presents this serious subject like an old radio drama probing events in history like the Scopes "monkey" trial, Robert Ripley's "Believe it or Not," Ralph Ellison's *Invisible Man* and Rachel Carson's *Silent Spring*. In the style of a private eye, the historian investigates how we got to this "post-truth" moment in history—a kind of *Twilight Zone* of twisted reality.

The seriousness of this truth-killing mystery is sharpened in Michael Eric Dyson's book, *What Truth Sounds Like*. Dyson takes us into a New York City apartment in 1963 for the historic meeting of Robert F. Kennedy, James Baldwin, Lena Horne, Harry Belafonte and other Black voices. Kennedy was confronted with the truth—many troubling truths—regarding the experience of Black Americans. "Schools, churches, social clubs, businesses and courts were run by and for white folks," and Kennedy believed there was a political solution. What he heard in that room was harder to hear. As Dyson explains near the end of the book: *"[This] meeting with a few angry black folk more than fifty years ago taught him a valuable lesson about listening to* what you don't want to hear. It is a lesson we must learn today if we are to overcome our differences and embrace a future as bright as our dreams allow."

This reality check can be very disorienting—like truth itself. The implications for religious faith and secular humanism are profound. The challenge is to be honest about how committed we are to the perpetual search for the true, the good, the real. Like RFK, we may need to let go of controlling the narrative, what we think should be in the center of the table in the middle of the room. As with so many other areas of faith, we have to return to the essential yet disturbing practice of listening.

Did the founders of religious traditions practice good listening? We have selected portions of what they may have spoken, but how often were they simply listening to the questions, the discontent, the anger of others? Those pregnant pauses might have been more instructive than their words, though it would reveal that perhaps Moses or Jesus, Buddha or Confucius, Krishna or Muhammad had more to learn—that they valued listening in their own search for truth.

No one individual embodies Truth. I'm well aware of the words attributed to Jesus in the *Gospel of John*: "I am the Way, the Truth and the Life." In our youthful evangelistic days we also preached, "The truth shall set you free," assuming that was also speaking of Jesus. Yet, no single person can embody all truth, nor can any religion, ideology, philosophy or nationality.

Scriptures imply they contain "The Truth," yet once again, the pursuit of what is true (and right and good) can never be printed, bound and published, because it is an active process of discovery followed by more discoveries. It's about building knowledge on basic humility. Whenever we hear truth or face truth, chances are it will cause a destabilizing disturbance.

In *What Truth Sounds Like*, Dyson speaks of the critical need for "witness." What bothered Robert Kennedy so much in that New York apartment was that he was surrounded by witnesses testifying to the injustices and feelings of hopelessness, caught in a culture deaf to their witness, denying their worth. Kennedy was engulfed in a circle of truth-tellers who surprised him with "the explosive power of truth through testimony." Over time, as Attorney General, Senator and presidential candidate, the truth became clearer, his education expanded.

As Dyson sees it, we can draw on those lessons even now—and we must. James Baldwin offers a difficult, perhaps dangerous, way forward. "Baldwin eventually concluded that it is possible to be true to one's individual imperatives while echoing the vision of others … ." Baldwin himself states this in the context of the artist: "It is the writer's necessity to deal as truthfully as possible with his own experience, and it is his hope to enlarge his experience to contain the experience of others, of millions" ("This Nettle, Danger"). Though we can't speak for others, we can make room for their voices to be heard.

Is this what truth looks like—making room, "listening spaces" for honest exchanges, common learning, common action? There may be "old truths" replaced by "new truths" but we are never post-truth.

3

Turtles, Snakes, Rabbits and the Human Race

Carol slowed to a stop in our neighborhood. Spying a black snake slithering across the pavement, she waited and watched, hoping no one would come speeding down the road. Minutes earlier she stopped behind a truck on a busy roadway. As a line of cars waited, a box turtle lumbered across to the lake.

We often feel concerned for the innocent, vulnerable creatures who suffer and die because of humans and our dangerous, speeding machines.

I wonder: do we need religions, religious teachers or scriptures to tell us to take life slower? Do we require reminders from ancient authors or whispers from heavenly voices to wake us up, to make us see we are not the only or the most important living things on this small planet?

Taking a walk with Carol's mother, we paused to notice the surroundings including bumps and cracks in the pavement. She uses a wheeled walker and moves slowly, deliberately, so we can't be in a hurry. We have to be patient, pay attention, try to see what my mother-in-law is seeing, or what she may not see, or hear. It's not easy to match our pace with another person, especially when we feel we have to get someplace else and time is constantly pushing or pulling us. If we can't let go of Time, from time to time, we miss so much, and that can be harmful.

No wonder we call ourselves the "Human Race." We have

such a hard time slowing, pausing, stopping, as we're racing somewhere for something. I'm amused the word "hurry" rhymes with "worry" as we "scurry" in a "flurry" of endless activity. What harm does this cause, to us, each other, our world? I think it's a good practice to pause and contemplate now and then, maybe often.

Many people move to our "neck of the woods" to live in beautiful surroundings. Western North Carolina is one great refuge, a world of living things, like us. The Blue Ridge Parkway is not merely an asphalt artery across the mountains but, as the name should remind us, a "park." That's unusual in the National Park system because it's a ribbon of land with a winding thread running through it. In other words, the Parkway is literally a Way through a Park—it's all one narrow wilderness park. It may not feel that way when cars are speeding along or packed into an overview, trailhead or visitors 'center, but that's the point here. There are distractions, and—here's an irony—even the views can be distracting and dangerous, drawing attention from living things close at hand.

What is an animal crossing the road potentially teaching us? "Getting there" seems vitally important, but "getting here" may be more valuable. Being alert, awake. I learned this truth from years of "presence ministry" with people in jail, on the streets and with many elders I've known. Mindful religious practice confirms this essential principle of life.

I worry a lot about the innocent and vulnerable, both human and non-human. Carol and I share a sensitivity to the suffering of others and it makes us angry sometimes. What can we do? How can we protect them? There's a feeling of helplessness. We see cars speeding through the neighborhood and cringe to think how many small living things are likely to be killed. We see people around the world, or on the streets of our towns, overlooked by human racing ... the hurried movements of people who don't notice and perhaps don't care.

As I was writing, a small, tawny rabbit hopped to the patio window; putting its paws on the glass, peering in at me. I was silently still and smiling. The bunny hopped to another window and did the same thing—an endearing natural curiosity. I sense the need to keep watching, on the lookout for what more wild neighbors are doing, near and far. Everything we do impacts their lives and, aware or not, what they are doing impacts us. Our environment is theirs too, maybe more theirs.

In the conclusion to her book, *Biomimicry*, biologist Janine Benyus speaks of "quieting" and "immersing ourselves in nature." Putting our noisy, hurrying humanity in perspective, she quotes Iroquois elder Oren Lyons on our equal standing with all of nature: "[We are living] between the mountain and the ant ... part and parcel of creation."

A word of wisdom we need to hear—a lesson of life crossing our path, something to slow us down. The voice of the elder and the voice of the scientist calling us back to the ground that belongs to the turtle on the road, the snake on the driveway, the rabbit at the window, and the more conscious human being.

4

Learning the Language of Humanity

From ninth grade through high school I took Spanish classes. Some of it was a comedy of errors and that first year was terrible, but Mr. Lundberg was patient and I finally began to catch on, finishing with a good grade and fairly good sense of the language. That encouraged me to continue studying Spanish with Ms. Cain for three years of senior high.

Choosing more impractical subjects (like theology) in college, I didn't continue Spanish, but backpacking around Europe after graduation took me to Germany, Switzerland, Italy, France and Spain. Staying in Barcelona and Madrid felt familiar as I recalled the history and culture from Spanish classes. It was satisfying to use some of what I learned in school, able to understand conversations, read signs and menus, and string words into imperfect but intelligible sentences.

There were many opportunities to practice my basic "Espanol" as a chaplain.

While serving as a jail chaplain in the SF Bay Area we saw a large number of ethnicities coming in and out the "revolving door" of incarceration (carcel: Spanish for jail). With a large immigrant population, many from Latin America, I spent countless hours listening to "broken" English and conversing in "broken" Spanish. Detainees appreciated that I would make the attempt to understand and converse.

We often had Spanish-speaking inmates attending weekly services, so I made feeble attempts to be bi-lingual. This caused puzzled expressions and laughter but also smiles and nods of gratitude—everyone could feel they were included. At least I was trying.

Roberto, from El Salvador, joined the group one evening and immediately helped translate the readings, songs and conversation. As I spoke with him at his cell during the week I sensed that he respected my attempts to communicate with other native Spanish speakers and I told him how grateful I was for his assistance. Roberto wrote out translations of readings and songs I would give him through the steel bars and by Sunday he would have copies for me. He didn't have much else to do with his time awaiting trial ... for murder.

Yolanda, from Guatemala, spoke little English but she attended the groups in the Women's Unit, singing, giggling and sometimes crying. She missed her children, which was easy to understand, no matter the language. Yolanda's joyful nature was contagious in the cell where we met with other women. I actually looked forward to those small circles, locked inside with "criminals" like Yolanda—most of whom had not been convicted of any crime.

In street chaplaincy we met even more people who spoke Spanish. Jose, from Mexico, was a kind and gentle man we first met in the free dining room downtown. He became a regular at our weekly Wellness group and Sunday circle in the park. Jose had a bright face and even brighter attitude though he lived "in the bushes" or under the freeway with a lot of people who shared his precarious situation with the difficult job of looking for work day after day.

Jose really made our day when he would appear at the chaplaincy office door with a big "sonrisa" (smile) and, frequently, "una palabra de sapiente" (a word of wisdom). That wisdom might simply be: "Tenemos no hogar, pero tenemos humanidad" (we have no home, but we have humanity). When we would tell him he was a wise man, Jose chuckled and replied, in English: "one thing I know —I know nothing" (I'm not sure he knew he was quoting Socrates).

If we were speaking with someone else, Jose would simply stand in the doorway quietly waiting. What was he waiting for? Connection, I suppose, with people who wouldn't judge him, chase him or arrest him. He would never fail to say, with a grin, "Thank You, Mucho!" Though he had nothing but the clothes on his back, Jose never asked for anything, unless it was for another person or to ask if any of us needed anything! He would help us move furniture or assist someone getting into our van to take them to the hospital, shelter or new apartment. He would assist in translating for another person, teach us a new word in Spanish or give us a lesson in a Latino custom.

My Spanish comprehension and conversation has grown rusty again with lack of practice. It's especially difficult to understand when a person talks a little too fast. But when we take the time to listen, really listen, I think we can understand just about anyone, in any language.

I'm not sure I ever fully appreciated the Spanish word "sonrisa" until I met Jose. His smile was in every way a "sunrise." And he gave us both his "corazon" (heart) and "presencia" (presence). A truly good-hearted hombre.

5

Still Points of History Along an Appalachian River

On a secular pilgrimage to Scotland some years ago, I parked my tiny rental car along the twisting road through Glencoe and set off to slog my way up to a high waterfall. I say "slog" because the spongey ground in those wilder places is, as the Scots say, "boggy." It's a given you'll get soaked. The land literally sinks into you as you sink into it. As I reached the gushing cascade spilling from the ancient rocks and gnarled trees, I was overcome with the emotion of "being home," though I had never before set foot in Scotland. Ancestors felt near, not as a ghostly presence but as a part of the land itself.

In his own kind of pilgrimage along the New River, Noah Adams maps out a land he sinks into as well. *Far Appalachia* tells a story made of many stories as he travels the 350-mile course of the New River from its source in North Carolina, passing north through Virginia to its end in West Virginia. Adams explores the country by driving, hiking, biking, canoeing and rafting. Born in eastern Kentucky, the writer has a deep sense this is his land and these are his people.

What struck me the most about Noah Adams' book is the respect he holds for the storytellers he meets and the way he meets them. The various modes of transportation he uses (particularly by boot, bike, canoe and raft) give his encounters a free-flowing nature. As he moves, he is moved by the individuals and their rooted relations with the river.

Adams doesn't say much about religion but he does describe how the church steeples mark the landscape and the lives of generations. He writes: "The churches of the small communities are the still points of history." He observes townsfolk standing on the steps of old parishes, sharing stories as they have for a very long time. He reflects, and moves on, with the river.

What impresses about a story like this is the central focus: nature—the mountains, the river, the forests, the people. So much stays the same; so much constantly changes. With these images in mind we can contemplate each still point along the never-still rivers we find.

The way we travel on our own personal "pilgrimage" makes a difference. If we only travel by "box" (car, train, plane) we miss so much. A glimpse and glance, a stop here and there, passing people and places that potentially offer the stories we most need to hear and feel. Bicycles and boats can bring another depth of experience. Walking or hiking open even more. Yet none of these will get us any closer to the natural world and the lives of inhabitants unless we sense the need for both still points and streams ahead, to have courage to go further, to see beyond ourselves. *Far Appalachia* reminds us of that wisdom.

This wise approach connects to my own still points and wanderings through spirituality and beyond. Where can I still find stillness to reflect on my history and the history of "the people"?

Sometimes it feels I've only traveled a few miles on the river, heard only a handful of stories. Other times it feels like I've soaked in too much, streams of stories, thoughts and beliefs have merged into a big muddy river—the bogginess has me bogged down, soaked and sunken.

We might all relate to the obstacles Noah Adams encounters on his journey through the mountains. There are storms, of course, as well as rapids, falls, boulders, fences and a few people. At one point his cycling is hampered by a No Trespassing sign. While canoeing and rafting, he needs a guide to help steer around immovable obstacles. To find our own passages to places of stillness, guides may help.

The goal might be to reach the end of the river, yet the river flows on into other rivers. The river's journey has no end, even when its waters mingle and spill out into the sea. We set our goals and destinations, but even if we reach those points, how many destinations have we passed or missed? This is a lesson in knowing which river is before us and beneath us, aware of where we stand, where we're going, across a historical landscape much greater than we. If some say that river is divine, I see no reason to be an obstacle in their way. For others like me, a "new" river presents a delightful opportunity to move, change, grow, explore. We always know there are rivers coursing through other mountains beyond. If we discover our own still points, maybe we'll learn to know the nearest river, even within.

6

In the Galaxy of Religion, Resistance is Not Futile

In the Sci-Fi series, "Star Trek: The Next Generation," one of the most dangerous aliens is the Borg—a species that travels in huge black cubes, "assimilating" all other species they encounter. The Borg captures anyone in their path and turns each organism into a half-organic/half-mechanized hybrid. With humans this means a person is transformed into a machine, part by part. Frightening, horrible. "You will be assimilated" is the most fearsome thing the crew of the Enterprise hears as they cross the galaxy.

In their persistent quest to stop the Borg, the starship crew tries everything. Finding they can't outrun the Borg or hide from them, they hit the big powerful cubes with massive firepower, but nothing works; there seems no way to avoid being absorbed into the predator network. The Borg is a "collective"—like a mammoth bee hive—that operates as one, each part working in sync with the other. Unless a species chooses to join the collective (and no one would), the voice from the Borg booms out: "Resistance is futile." And for most species in space, it is.

So how does the Enterprise finally stop the Borg? They find a way to separate one of the "bees" from the "hive" and show him, through human kindness and friendship, that he is an "individual" with a mind of his own. He discovers he can think for himself and freely choose whether to go back to being a "drone" or a self-determining person.

I won't spoil the whole story, but the moment "Hugh" says "I think" rather than "We think," everything changes, for him, and for the Borg.

See any connection to religious faith here? Not only religion, of course, but any "hive," any group or party that seeks to incorporate individuals into a collective. To operate efficiently, the machine requires obedient members who cooperate as a single unit. The machine won't function if too many decide they don't want to be cogs any longer. "I think" can be the greatest threat to the corporate machines.

For a great many people in history, resisting the collective has been futile. They feel powerless to disconnect from the overpowering control of the Great Cubes. When people are led to believe the Cube is invincible, that assimilation is inevitable, they give up their power with their individuality.

On the other hand, we might find a positive element to the cube collective. A bee hive can be a highly efficient community working together for the benefit of all. If every individual unit is able to follow their instinct for preservation and production (honey), the hive thrives. Of course, bees aren't evangelizing other bees or other species—they go about their business and don't bother anyone who doesn't bother them.

Yet, we're not bees (or ants, or a herd). If we become drones living only to serve the Queen (the Almighty Authority), some good can certainly come from that—a well-ordered society ... and honey! Yet, how many drones know they are drones? And, is the Queen (the ultimate leader, perhaps a deity) benevolent, or is it malevolent and abusive?

To resist means to stand and withstand. Resistance is not futile, though sometimes it seems that way. An individual, or a coalition, pushes back on the power of the impersonal Cube and they meet resistance from the Cube. In order not to be forced into a collective where we lose our precious individuality we have to stand and insist on resistance.

The crew of the Enterprise discovered a weakness in the Great Machine that threatened their freedom. The search for the underbelly of the Borg presented a response, a clear way to resist. The word "futile" comes from a word for "leaky"—literally, something can't hold water, it's useless, pointless. In matters of belief, futility means giving up the will to resist, giving in to a "greater power." If that greatness can be found in a creative and constructive collective, where each is valued, that's not futile. Who would resist that?

Though we have a right to resistance, we don't need to resist positive change.

The National Park Service is faced with some difficult decisions about which lands to protect. In new guidelines, park managers are being asked "to think beyond resistance to change and begin considering transformation" (*The New York Times*, "What to Save?," May 18, 2021). Priorities may need to be re-ordered to take a stand to benefit all.

Concerning the religious enterprise, people of faith can stand alongside secular people to transform our world for good, insisting on individual autonomy and resisting Cube-thinking. We need many voices among the crew, in a circle not a cube, where a galaxy of perspectives are assimilated.

7

Who Holds the Keys to the Kingdom, or Safe Sanctuaries?

As a high school youth group leader I went to the pastor and asked if we could have access to the church during the week when no one was there. He didn't seem to care that I was a seventeen-year-old growing my hair and beard long, wearing jeans that dragged on the ground. Knowing we were "Jesus Freaks" who loved to sing, study and pray, he seemed to have no worries. He handed me a set of keys.

It felt good to be so trusted. Pastor Mudge was a bit quirky and most of the time the youth liked that. When he brought a record player into the sanctuary and played pop songs during his sermon, I think our parents were mildly amused. He had some rather liberal views on the Bible and theology, but told good stories that pleased most of the congregation in our small Presbyterian church near Seattle.

His hair was a little longer than a pastor's hair should be (traditionally speaking), and with his bushy eyebrows and big laugh, he was a down-to-earth kind of "God guy."

As we were drawn into the evangelism of Campus Crusade, we wondered sometimes if Pastor Mudge was even "saved." That kind of doubt over everyone's salvation seemed to drive our desperate attempts to bring our world to Christ. But thankfully, most of us outgrew that need to make others believe our beliefs.

The youth group scattered to college, work or military service and most of us lost track of each other. After four years of studying Religion and Philosophy in a local Christian university, I came back to speak with pastor Mudge.

Bruce (as an adult now, I was pleased to be more familiar) was happy to hear I was considering ministry and suggested I take a look at the seminary in California where he received his Masters degree. On his recommendation, I made the journey down the coast and spent the next four years becoming a "master of divinity" which, for many of us, culminated with a "call" to a church position where we would be entrusted with a new set of keys.

You've probably heard of "The Keys of the Kingdom." This comes from Matthew 16 where Jesus asks his disciples if they know who he is. Peter answers: "You are the Chosen One, the Child of the Living God." Right answer. He's handed the keys. What will those keys do? To paraphrase: "Whatever you lock on earth will be locked in heaven. Whatever you unlock on earth will be unlocked in heaven." The Catholic Church has taken this to mean the Pope—who stands in the shoes of Peter, the fisherman—carries those old keys in his pastoral pocket. He can lock and unlock whatever he wishes, guarding the gilded gates for God.

I don't know about that, but there is something powerful and empowering about having keys. To be able to lock and unlock doors (or turn machines on or off) carries the weight of responsibility.

Receiving your first set of keys to a car, a classroom, a janitor's closet, a new apartment—you feel important having the ability to go in and out anytime you want.

Thinking back to the day pastor Mudge handed me those church keys, trusting me with that awesome responsibility, I still have gratefulness for his support and encouragement in those wild youthful times. Where would I have ended up if Bruce and others in the church, college and the seminary hadn't seen some glimmer of leadership ability in me?

Who are your voices of encouragement, your teachers, your mentors? Are they all in the past or are their voices present? Did they hand on any useful keys?

What keys do we carry? What keys are we entrusted with? Where do we have access? How do we handle that responsibility?

As a youth leader I would open the church building any time day or night. If some of us felt like praying, singing or hanging out, we knew there was a quiet space open and available. Our parents didn't always know, and I doubt most members knew, when we were inside "God's House." How many youth feel they have access to that kind of safe, welcoming space today? And, it's worth thinking about if you're a believer: how many of "God's Houses" are locked tight by the keyholders when so many are in need of being inside other than Friday night or Sunday morning?

What's the key to all this? I think of our move away from handheld keys to pushbuttons, fingerprint or eye scans. Keys are changing.

Who really holds the "keys to the kingdom"—locking and unlocking the "sacred spaces"?

Maybe everyone. Maybe no one.

8

Wonder is Wonder, Breathing is Breathing (and Presence is Presence)

You may have a similar experience—I read an article, hear an interview, watch a film or have an engaging conversation and my brain starts making connections to ideas or words from various sources. It's usually a good indication I need to think more about a topic, ask questions, and maybe write.

In the Summer 2021 issue of "The Humanist," I read an article by Daniel Moran, one of the magazine's editors: "Art and the Nature of Spirituality." Readers and students familiar with my suspicion of slippery spiritual semantics and my peculiar personal secular view of nature, won't be surprised to hear I had a reaction. As a humanist like me who does not hold theistic beliefs, the author seems to know what he's doing. Yet when the waters of religion are already so murky, I see no reason to stir them and make them even muddier.

Moran suggests using the word "spirituality" does not present a conflict for non-theists. In fact, he contends it is "a necessary part of a full life." His view is that spirituality identifies the ways we connect with the deepest parts of our humanity and "how we see this connectedness to the wonders and mysteries of the world around us." The example he uses is love. "We know what love is because it is part of our spirituality." He rightly traces the word spirituality to its original meaning: to breathe (actually wind, breath), then presents what he thinks best expresses this breathing: art.

In art, particularly his sense of poetry, this author finds beauty, meaning, fulfillment and wonder. This is what it means to be human, he says, "in this universal scheme of grandeur and mystery." He concludes with a kind of breathable benediction: "Breathe, and breathe deeply."

While I can appreciate where he's coming from, I find myself a little puzzled by this perspective. When I hear a fellow freethinker defend this use of old language I feel constrained to push back a bit. I know it's not necessarily a big deal when we turn to familiar words to express ourselves, yet there is one point of contention I would raise.

If we're talking about taking a deep breath of appreciation, gratitude … or air …, what is the purpose in calling it something other than those things, especially when there's a long history with some words we use? For most people acculturated in religious terminology, faith-flavored terms evoke belief in the supernatural. Yet, wonder is wonder, beauty is beauty, breathing is breathing—all good (good is good too). Why pull natural words out of a holy hat or a bag of beliefs labeled "spirituality"?

Boston doctor, Daniela Lamas, wrote about one of her Covid patients who had a remarkable recovery ("What Should Doctors Do When We Experience a Miracle?," NYT, July 2, 2021). *"[That] night, my team watched in amazement as his oxygen levels started to rise, slowly at first and then steadily. Standing outside his room, I found myself, somewhat uncomfortably, thinking of miracles. As a critical-care doctor, I become nervous at the very idea of miracles. I hear the word and think of tense family meetings and impossible hopes. I im-*

agine loved ones at the bedside waiting for improvement that will never come. Miracles are often what patients' families beg for, and they're not something that I can provide."

The doctor is faced with a difficult question: "What does it mean for a miracle to happen in the intensive care unit?" She knows how intertwined the word miracle is with religious faith, so she reasons: *"I am not invoking the spiritual or the supernatural. As doctors in training, we attend entire lectures to help us navigate conversations with families who are waiting for divine intervention to bring their loved one back from the brink. What I am interested in is how we deal with the one-in-a-million outcomes, the patients who surprise and humble us."*

With this particular patient, the doctor stays true to her compassionate secular view. When another patient did not recover, the doctor was honest with the family: "There would be no miracle, but perhaps there would be peace. It was time to say goodbye." The physician's presence was a deep breath of human kindness.

As humanist artist Daniel Moran sees it, we experience "grandeur and mystery" through our natural artistry. I would say this shows how intimately our nature is integrated with Nature itself. It seems to me we can enjoy the fulfillment of our humanity without resorting to lighter-than-air words that only add more confusion.

We may be surprised and humbled to discover the "miraculous and spiritual" is as natural as our own breath and the thoughtful presence of another.

9

Shakers, Trappists, and the Inclusive Dance of Simplicity

My wife, a Presbyterian minister, drove with me, her freethinking Humanist spouse (and former Presbyterian minister), to spend a few days at Pleasant Hill, Kentucky. We stayed in the "Farm Deacon's" stone house, a restored 200-year-old dwelling in a historic village founded by a community who saw themselves as the true Church of Christ—the "United Society of Believers in Christ's Second Appearing," who believed they were "not of this world." We know them as Shakers. And, essentially, they are no longer of this world.

The Shakers held a radical, but not unusual, millenial doctrine. Christ was returning very soon and they needed to be prepared. John Dunlavy (1769-1826) was a Presbyterian minister who converted to Shakerism and lived at Pleasant Hill where he wrote, "The Manifesto, or, A declaration of the doctrines and practice of the Church of Christ." The treatise presents the biblical origins of the Shaker belief in the imminent return of Christ and how His special people should prepare for the heavenly journey. When that didn't happen (Adventists, Witnesses and other groups had a similar experience of disappointment), the Shakers settled down to a quiet, communal farming life, eventually fading from history. Yet, their village and philosophy of simplicity remain.

From Shaker Village we drove to Gethsemani Abbey where

monk and writer Thomas Merton once lived. Merton wrote: "The Shakers believed that the conventional organized 'churches 'had been reduced to ... complicity with the world ... money ... and an appetite for power." When active in un-conventional chaplaincy, I was impressed with Merton's interfaith work bringing together Buddhists, Jews, Muslims, Hindus and Christian monastics in dialogue.

In the Gethsemani chapel we sat in silence listening to the brothers chanting afternoon prayers. A beautiful, peaceful place for contemplation. After prayers, as the monks walked passed us, I observed a curious thing. Not one of the forty brothers smiled or glanced in our direction, giving nary a nod to acknowledge our presence. Now, I fully understand that monastic life, particularly Trappist, emphasizes silence, contemplative work and separation from the world. I retain some respect for that, even as a secular person. There can be value in living close to the land and doing the "inner work," centered in a simple life of poverty However, I was struck by the irony of chanting praise and offering prayers for the human family while seeming to ignore guests. Would we distract the brothers from their communion with God?

This somewhat disappointing experience led me back to Merton, who often prayed in that chapel. He concluded his book, *New Seeds of Contemplation*, with an invitation to an inclusive dance: "We are invited to forget ourselves on purpose, cast our awful solemnity to the winds and join in the general dance."

I compared this experience at the Abbey with the Shaker community. They too separated from "worldly" influences yet also invited observers into their Meeting Halls to join in singing and dancing for hours of joyful music and movement. I've known enough priests, monks and nuns to be aware and appreciative of the diversity of practices within Christian contemplative traditions. This helps balance my limited experience with the Shakers and Trappists.

Returning to Shaker Village, a young Black woman interpreter invited our group of visitors to sing and dance in the Meeting Hall, reminding us how Shakers included women and people of color. Then we entered the large stone Centre Family house, fascinated by the architecture, furniture and the Shaker story itself. I stood staring into the faces of children in a large photo before reading of one influential individual in the early movement—John Whitbey (1792-1843). An interpretive plaque read: "John Whitbey's logical and rational approach to life drew him to the Shakers, but his free-thinking personality and writings ultimately rattled Pleasant Hill. Whitbey viewed Shaker elders as well-intentioned people but questioned their claim to divine inspiration." He eventually wrote a personal account of Shakerism that "caused some Believers to question their faith, plaguing the Shakers for years to come." Ah, the danger of freethought!

This is a stumbling stone for those who can't wait to exit this dark dance floor for the bright ballroom above. What do you do when you're earthbound, stuck in the secular— the present world? You eagerly await the end, the flight to heaven, yet the promises and prayers fall unfulfilled. You either separate yourself from the human family and dance (pray, study scripture, etc) among yourselves, or you join the greater dance where everyone is welcome.

Shakers and Trappists offer something for our world, this world. And if the practices, piety and prayers cannot create an open circle for dancing, we can simply enjoy a silent (or singing) appreciation for the unshaken beauty of our world.

10

Thomas Merton, Shakers and the Paradise Myth

Mother Ann Lee, founding matriarch of the community known as Shakers, brought her message from England to the New World in the 1770's. The "New World" she and her small entourage of believers sought was beyond America (beyond this world!), but it began here. Mother Ann once said: "There is no dirt in heaven," yet she envisioned American soil perfect for planting paradise.

At Pleasant Hill, the restored Shaker Village near Lexington, Kentucky, we picked up a copy of Thomas Merton's *Seeking Paradise: The Spirit of the Shakers*. As a Cistercian (Trappist) monk living at Gethsemani Abbey not far from Pleasant Hill, Merton was keenly curious about this early heretical community. He understood the term "Shaker" referred not only to the joyous dancing in their Meeting Houses but to the way the spirit would seem to be "shaking the whole community in a kind of prophetic earthquake." They believed their movement would "shake" the world in preparation for the return of Christ.

While awaiting that End Time, the Shakers worked the land and concentrated their efforts on crafting beautiful buildings and furniture. Their unique craftsmanship was, according to Merton, "not only a manifestation of their practicality but a witness to their common faith. Indeed one is tempted to say that it is a better, clearer, more comprehensible expression of their faith than their written theology was." Merton goes on to state: "The inspired Shaker simplicity, the reception of simplicity as a charismatic gift, as a sign of truth and of salvation, is powerfully and silently eloquent in the word of their hands." What they did, what they made with their own hands, and even their silence, spoke more loudly than their beliefs. What they created was who they were, it embodied their belief —a silent eloquence. As Merton later wrote: "This wordless simplicity, in which the works of quiet and holy people speak humbly for themselves. How important that is for our day ... ." In the mind of the monk, "The Shakers remain as witnesses to the fact that only humility keeps [humankind] in communion with truth, and first of all with their own inner truth."

Mother Ann planted many words of wisdom. "Do be truthful; do avoid exaggeration." "Whatever is really useful is virtuous though it does not at first seem so." "Order is the creation of beauty." Even with this simple wisdom and gentle lifestyle, the Shakers were misunderstood and persecuted. As earthly time passed, celibate and not celebrated, their tools were laid down in the shops, buildings abandoned, dancing ceased (the last two aged Shakers live at Sabbathday Lake in Maine). Yet the simple, silent eloquence of their craft lives on.

In 1962, Merton was invited to an exhibition of Shaker drawings but couldn't attend. In a letter to an organizer, Mary Childs Black, he wrote: "Their spirit is perhaps the most authentic expression of the primitive American 'mystery' or 'myth': the paradise myth." The Shaker community sought to return to the Garden of Eden and create a kind of heaven on earth, yet also set their hopes on a heavenly meeting place above. They presented an alternative to "the secular vision of the earthly paradise" where "the Indian had been slaughtered and the Negro was enslaved [and] the immigrant was treated as an inferior being." The new world they imagined was radically different than the prevailing myth of an American paradise. Shakers believed in "something totally original about the spirit and the vocation of America."

Merton concludes his admiring reflections on Shakerism in his letter to Mary Childs Black with his own startled, and perhaps sad, realization. The Shakers not only saw the potential of America to be a new Eden, they worked, they existed, to make it so. And, "The sobering thing is that their vision was eschatological! And they themselves ended." With their faith in a heavenly paradise, their eyes on the garden above, they became absorbed by the land, part of the gardens, orchards and fields of Kentucky, Maine and elsewhere. Merton quotes another writer who asserted there was "an atmosphere of settledness" among the Shakers, "as though they were part of the land itself." How many religious communities share that intimate relationship with the earth?

There is a certain sadness, or disappointment, when we consider the Shakers. For me, it's similar to the description of some in the early Christian church, experimenting with a new community, living by the words of Jesus. No one was isolated, no one suffered alone—"no one in need." And extending this beyond Christianity, beyond religion itself, who are the ones "shaking" our world today? Are we able to hear their "silent eloquence"? Who is in need? Who shares a dream of building (or recognizing) paradise here today?

11

Symbols and Statues of Liberty and Responsibility

Symbols reveal the best and the worst of our nature. We show honor, respect, even reverence, for some images, especially those that remind us who we are, where we came from, who helped get us to where we are. Then, we often fight over those very questions.

In an article on the Statue of Liberty published July Fourth weekend, culture critic Philip Kennicott discussed the history of the iconic image standing over New York harbor ("Maybe it's time to admit that the Statue of Liberty has never quite measured up," *The Washington Post*, July 3, 2021). He explains that in the 1870's the concept was to have broken chains in the hands of Lady Liberty. Apparently that symbol of the end of slavery was too much for some. The chain idea was replaced by the tablet with 1776 on it. Iron chains or not, ironies abound. The statue was a woman, though women weren't free to vote, and Chinese laborers helped build the base of the statue, though the Chinese Exclusion Act loomed over their heads.

Some Catholic groups were upset about the statue because she was: "Holding her torch to proclaim that mankind receives true light, not from Christ and Christianity, but from heathenism and its gods."

There came a moment when Kennicott realized: "a statue that held little meaning to me was suddenly meaningful in a very particular way: I could reject it." As Frederick Douglass said of Independence Day, in his speech on July 5, 1852, Kennicott had to say: "This is your symbol, not mine." He is not only taking a personal political stand with this. It's about liberty and liberation. As he states so succinctly: "It may well be that there is more genuine liberty embodied in the rejection of a symbol than the acceptance of it. And that raises a curious question about the United States: Why are we so obsessed not just with national symbols, but with the utterly unlikely prospect that we will all accept and honor these symbols in exactly the same way?"

When the most important symbol in my life, the Cross, splintered and fell, it shook the ground of my faith. Like all old wood, it dissolved into the soil and I found myself in a ploughed field of secular spirituality. After a few years, the field of cross-shaped crops transformed into a meadow of wildflowers encircled by the forests of faith. Or something like that. I'm reaching for descriptors to help understand the movement, the shift from under the shadow of a symbol.

I'm very aware this is a sensitive subject. Sometimes we have to listen to voices that make us uncomfortable. Visiting the website of the United Daughters of the Confederacy, I was a little startled to read these words from the President General of that organization: "We are grieved that certain hate groups have taken the Confederate flag and other symbols as their own." She goes on to explain: "The United Daughters of the Confederacy totally denounces any individual or group that promotes racial divisiveness or white supremacy. And we call on these people to cease using Confederate symbols for their abhorrent and reprehensible purposes." I wasn't expecting that. We may be skeptical about motives, and may have strong feelings, but sometimes there are cracks in the monuments that memorialize our beliefs, living or dead. Even the smallest of agreements could hold potential for dialogue, perhaps progress.

Walking through the beautiful Ashland park surrounding famous statesman Henry Clay's home in Lexington, Kentucky, we saw a marker commemorating a victory by rebel troops across from an interpretive sign about the enslaved people who worked that land. Symbols of our dilemma: we are people who have a mixed story, intertwined stories, and we're still torn by how to tell a common story, and if there is one. A serious study of our honest history seems to be the best way forward, if we can agree on that, and that won't be easy.

I often recall something psychologist Viktor Frankl, a survivor of Nazi Germany, said. There is a statue of **Liberty** on the East Coast. We ought to have a statue of **Responsibility** on the West Coast. That's the necessary balance, and our symbols can be a powerful image for that balance. Personal liberty is a necessary right, but it has to be weighed in the scale of responsibility to others. The greatest religious teachings point to this.

If our symbols become idols, or we refuse to think hard about them, to be self-critical, then it's no longer about the liberty to think for ourselves. We are "herd" because we have not heard the voices of those harmed by our idolized symbols.

If together we hold the torch higher, we may see farther down the road of liberty.

12

Is It True All Religions Worship the Same God?

Having devoted most of my vocational life to interfaith work, building relationships among people of various religious beliefs and worldviews, I gravitate to stories that reflect that positive side of religion.

In the Pacific Northwest county where I lived half my life, a new mosque is opening in a beautiful country setting. A Muslim leader said: "Sometimes, you forget to see the beauty that is all around us ... I can see God easily through his work." (*HeraldNet*, Everett, Washington, July 26, 2021). This feeling is understandable in that region given the deep green forests, clear rivers and snow-capped mountains in virtually all directions. In my early years I would have said the same thing—natural beauty and supernatural belief sometimes converge like the creeks.

Representatives of diverse faith traditions and other community leaders were invited to celebrate the end of Ramadan at the site of the new mosque. A faith leader described the intent: "Respect finds its true meaning when you're able to respect people who see the world with a different perspective, people you may think are wrong."

Another faith leader at the ceremony remarked: "We all worship the same God." At a later stage of my winding and wandering faith journey I would have said this too. Don't believers, especially in the "Abrahamic" traditions—

Judaism, Christianism, Islam—essentially follow the same deity? And if Hindus, Mormons, Buddhists, Sikhs and Taoists reverence one High God or Creative Force in the universe, don't they worship an identical divinity in different forms —the many faces or "masks" of God?

But not all creeks converge, do they? Not all rivers flow into the same lake or sea. And not every trail leads up the same mountain. In his important book, *God is Not One*, Stephen Prothero, professor of Religion at Boston University, makes this point clear: "The world's religious rivals do converge when it comes to ethics, but they diverge sharply on doctrine, ritual, mythology, experience, and law. These differences may not matter to mystics or philosophers of religion, but they matter to ordinary religious people" (Prothero is also the author of *Religious Literacy*). He goes on to explain the claim that all religions are one "is neither accurate nor ethically responsible. God is not one. Faith in the unity of religions is just that—faith."

This view presents some uncomfortable challenges to respected teachers such as the Dalai Lama or scholars such as Huston Smith. It's one thing to bring various representatives together to dialogue or even collaborate on specific projects that reflect similar ethical commitments. It's quite another thing to extrapolate from this that the religions are basically the same.

This recalls Wilma Dykeman's description of the French Broad river whose source in Western North Carolina (near Devil's Courthouse!) is both the North Fork and the Big Pigeon rivers. "Though they rise less than a mile apart, the French Broad does not receive this second largest tributary for almost a hundred and fifty miles and in another state [Tennessee]" (*The French Broad*, 1955). Are these rivers the same? Does the fact they meet up and flow together at a later juncture allow us to conclude that since they have a common destination therefore they are "one river"? Not at all.

The Muslim leader at the new mosque said some people in the surrounding community were unhappy and unwelcoming; they started a letter-writing campaign to stop the mosque. He feels these angry and fearful people simply don't know them, the congregation, or Islam (a usual issue with any interfaith work—people are either willing to learn, or not). And part of the learning for all of us is to admit we don't know that much about all these belief systems and it's up to us to choose to meet those with different beliefs. If we choose not to "cross the line" of difference, that's on us—we have no place judging the "other" if we don't know them.

This is the balance, isn't it? The religions are not the same, the gods are not the same, and it doesn't help to run them all together into a big bubbling river. Religion is not one peak of piety but a mountain range (with many valleys). We can appreciate the variety of rivers, mountains and paths, willing to face the fact of faith's diversity. As I see it, healthy, non-fear-based religion seeks the similarities and values the differences too. Streams, like mountains, must be viewed individually. Yes, it's all water, land—individual and communal experience of meaningful life and ethical living—but each one may consist of many paths, myriad streams. And each must be critically considered. Not every stream offers pure water; every mountain need not be ascended.

13

How Do We Know What an Atheist Believes?

Do you know any atheists? How would you know that you know any? They would have to say so. What makes a nonbeliever in a god or gods (the clearest definition of an atheist) any different from a believer in a god or gods? Probably not much. Observe what each is doing with their lives. I would guess there is no other way of knowing if a person believes in God or not unless they tell us.

My issue with atheism is that it doesn't tell me anything about a person. I am a man—not a "non-woman." I am an American—not a "non-citizen-of-every-other-country." You get the point. To declare "I am not one of those," is virtually meaningless. To go around claiming a negative—a NOT: "Not OF Them"—gives me almost zero information. Almost zero. When someone says they are an atheist, I learn they have concluded there is no divine supernatural being or reality. But that's all they have told me. I've learned nothing about who they are, what that god-decision means for them in their life, if it guides them to act differently than anyone else. I may assume things based on my personal feelings about atheism, but these are purely assumptions. Strange to say, I'd have to admit I'm an "agnostic" as to who they are. I simply don't know.

We can ponder these same questions with anyone who claims just about anything. "I am a believer in liberty." What does that mean? "I love chocolate but I don't eat meat." Do I know you better now? "I am a Christian." Well, now we're in trouble. This literally tells me nothing, except it's apparently important for you to assert that identity. Yet, it only raises many questions you may not be prepared for. Maybe you say you are "non-denominational" (which in itself has become a denomination, a sect of the Christian religion). Or you believe Jesus was a social reformer but not necessarily son of god. Would other "Christians" judge you "Christian"?

Roy Speckhardt, director of the American Humanist Association, questions what practical difference it makes what one believes about a Creator when making life decisions. "The label chosen to represent oneself will certainly impact public perceptions, but the practical implications are the same for atheists, agnostics and deists" (*Creating Change Through Humanism*). Greg Epstein, Humanist Chaplain at Harvard, has written that "the single biggest weakness of modern atheism and Humanism has been ... the movement's own tendency to focus on religious beliefs, when the key to understanding religion lies not in belief at all but in practice—in what people do, not just what they think" (*Good Without God*).

Stephen Prothero, professor of religion at Boston University, includes a chapter on atheism in his book on world religions, *God is Not One*. He challenges contemporary non-religious people to move beyond the angry, "evangelical," mostly white, male "New Atheists" to embrace a friendlier, more reasonable "new New Atheism." In Prothero's view, instead of trying to convert believers into atheists, we should have a common hope "for a world in which children can play with other children without regard for the religious (or non-religious) beliefs of their parents." And, as astrophysicist Neil deGrasse Tyson has stated, though he's agnostic about a Creator-God (he sees no evidence for one), he doesn't call himself an atheist. As a scientist, he thinks if the current mysteries of the universe are evidence for God, then "God is an ever-receding pocket of scientific ignorance" (interview with Bill Moyers, 2014). This "God of the Gaps" is forever the Unknown.

Am I an atheist? I don't believe I am (just joking). From my perspective, there is no divine being or anything supernatural, so it would be accurate to say that I am a nontheist. Yet, most of the time I choose not to call myself an atheist. "Freethinker" or "humanist" is my preferred, positive way of expressing how I view the world, what I believe as a secular person, since *believing isn't the point*. I "think" and "feel" it's right to be good—to be kind, compassionate and respectful—to others. I don't "believe" that's right and good. It makes reasonable sense to me. I suppose this is a matter of emphasis, or simply semantics, but it seems much more than that. Until both theists and non-theists can agree that being better humans together is the fundamental issue, the merry-go-round of BOBs will keep spinning. You know, BOBs? Those are the *Bubbles of Beliefs* that so many of us get trapped inside.

For my part, if I'm honest and a true freethinker, I have a few BOBs myself.

14

Suffering, Stuffering and Stumbling through Sickness

I read of a megachurch pastor who contracted Covid. As he recovered, his mother thanked people for praying for him: "Your prayers have been answered!" A usual, natural response. And of course this makes me wonder: if their prayers are so effective, why aren't more people recovering? Well, that's how my mind works.

An older relative of mine is suffering through a serious illness. He's never been very communicative in the past, so I didn't expect to hear much from him during his struggles. When he replied to my email, I was pleasantly surprised. True to form, his humor is still alive and well, telling me: "Thanks for the mention and thoughts on my stuff, but it's just stuff, and minimal stuffering." "Stuffering"—good old Highland word-playful humor. My relative followed up with: "No medical advice nor suggestions permitted." I suppose this is another Highland family trait, a nice way to say: I appreciate your concern, but don't bother me with what you think I should do. Not asking for anything, perhaps especially, no platitudes like "thoughts and prayers." He knows I was, once-upon-a-faith, a believer and a minister, so maybe he imagines I'd want to bring religion into his place of pain. I don't.

He and I recently lost a special family member who was 95 years old. When my relative responded to my feelings of loss, he shared the same thought: "I still think I should call to check in on her." That's our connection—the desire to connect, to stay in relation with a relative. What's family for, anyway, but an abiding presence of thoughtfulness and love?

As a secular humanist, I would pray for him, but I don't pray. I would believe he'll get better, but I don't believe. I would tell him he just needs to trust God, but I don't trust that, and wouldn't expect him to. Some might think that's sad, that it shows greater love to do those things, believe those things, say those things. Yet, I learned through many years of ministry as well as misery—my own load of "stuffering"—that those things can add to the stuff, as well as the suffering. Here's how I see it.

I've reflected and written about prayer for a long time. As a minister and chaplain, I was constantly asked: "Pray for me." But prayer can add "stuff" to a situation that is often unnecessary. The same can be true with quoting from scriptures. Do we really need to hear words from thousands of years ago, or caring words from those who are present with us now?

If I spoke any words at all, I would ask: "So, what's happening with you? How are you feeling? What do you need right now?" Questions like that. Most people I worked with didn't need prayers—a hand from Someone else somewhere. Someone they couldn't see or hear or touch. The request for prayer was actually a non-verbal request: "Please just be with me. I'm hurting." Honest, truthful, real. If a person is comforted by the feeling that God (Spirit, a Higher Power) is present with them, I wouldn't try to convince them otherwise. Those feelings are natural, in a kind of super-natural way. However, I've consistently found that people aren't really asking for more "stuff"—not more to think about, not more words to say or things to believe.

The worst thing is when a sufferer is told the suffering is their fault and there is more "spiritual stuff" they must do. Awful. Many raised in religious traditions feel they aren't worthy enough anyway, which is one reason people ask for a clergyperson (a worthy-person) to pray on their behalf. "Intercession," as the old language puts it. The unconscious hope is that a "mediator" will stand in between them and God to communicate appropriately. They may think: "God surely hears a clergyperson more than me."

"Stuffering." I refuse to add to that. When one we care about is experiencing suffering, it is literally, physically and mentally, "their stuff." They are hurting; it's they who feel pain, fear, uncertainty. I don't need to stuff in my own stuff, what I think is important, what they "need" to hear.

When my grandmother was dying in the hospital while I was in high school, I sat at her bedside and read poetry to her. She had been a schoolteacher early in life and appreciated literature. As a young evangelical, I chose to read religious poems to her. She seemed comforted by that, though I wonder now if it mattered what I read to her. I was there, her grandson, reading by her bedside, present in her suffering. All else was stuff.

No one is stuff-free. But next time we check in on someone who is suffering, it may be good to leave stuff alone.

15

Yoruba: The Greatest Religion You've Never Heard of

When considering the various religious traditions around the world we can see how they adapt and transform in diverse environments. We might think of a tree transplanted from one soil to another. There is an abiding relation with the original roots, but in the new ground, in a new climate, the tree may become quite distinct, almost like another species. I drew this analogy from religion teacher Stephen Prothero's book, *God is Not One: The Eight Rival Religions That Run the World*. We shouldn't be surprised to find a faith tradition looking and acting very different when transplanted from Beijing to San Francisco, from Mumbai to Tokyo, from Jerusalem to New York or from Lagos to Rio.

Is the Christian tree the same here as it is in other countries, on other continents? Observing the countless species of that one faith in the United States should help us answer that. To be a Christian in America may not even resemble being a Christian in Asia or Africa. Though missionaries often try to convert people to their own sectarian beliefs, rituals and customs (even to conform to the same language, clothing and culture), indigenous people find ways to hold their own well-rooted, well-watered beliefs.

My own white male American "well-educated" bubble was popped while reading Prothero's book. I was startled, even a bit troubled, by another gap in my education (there are many). I had to revisit the question first presented in the World Religions course at my evangelical college: How many trees of faith are there, how many species of religion? We learned about Hinduism, Buddhism, Confucianism, Taoism, Judaism, Christianism, Islam, Sikhism, Jainism, Shintoism and Zoroastrianism. "Animism" was mentioned as a more "primitive" form of religion, because the focus was on the "Great Religions"—meaning the oldest and most populous.

Prothero devotes a whole chapter on a major religious tradition I had barely heard of: Yoruba. This West African religion is very old and has millions of followers around the planet, especially in Nigeria, Brazil (where it's known as Candomble), Cuba (called Santeria) and elsewhere. It becomes quite obvious: indigenous religions are far older, more deeply rooted, than any of the so-called "Great" traditions.

In the Yoruba worldview, "orishas," are female and male spirits who influence human lives. Orishas have personalities and can be both creative and destructive, healing or harmful. Not exactly like the gods of Olympus, orishas live in the earth and they can suffer like humans. They are interested in putting humans in touch with a sacred power called "ashe." Prothero explains one of the best definitions of ashe is "the power to make things happen." It can simply be like saying "Amen—so be it." "Ifa," a form of divination (to "divine" the will of the spirits), is performed by priests and priestesses who assist the devoted in connecting to their sacred power and to Nature. In my limited understanding I would say this is like helping someone find the outlet to plug into the power source. A central focus of Yoruba is to re-connect people to their ashe.

It's hard to say how many gods there are in Yoruba, but the highest of them all is Olodumare. Western thinkers may have a hard time wrapping their minds around the fact that Olodumare is not the creator of the world and has no temples or priests. As there is no official scripture or theology in Yoruba, we can simply say Olodumare is Power itself. Nothing simple about that.

Fresh out of college I taught my first class on World Religions in my home church near Seattle. The adult education course was a basic introduction with readings from the scriptures of various traditions. Though somewhat radical at that time, in that church, people seemed to follow their curiosity and engage harder, deeper thinking. We all raised questions no one could answer. After studying Philosophy, I found that "creative ignorance" delightful and fascinating. New ideas flavored with fresh questions! I was hungry for them. As a secular person I still enjoy new tastes; I want to learn: What is this new thing? Why have I never learned about it before?

It's clear to me I never learned about Yoruba because it sounds so strange and exotic—and so African and Latin American (so non-white). Besides, most North Americans have settled into a comfortable cultural Christianism and somehow think we already have all we need—a god, a bible, plenty of churches, plenty of rituals and holidays.

Knowledge of Yoruba might help us turn up the dimmer switch in our minds. Can we connect with a greater power than the "Great Religions" have handed to us? What could that power-source be?

16

Jesus, John Wayne and Militant Masculinity

In the 1990's some guys like me were reading books by wise thinkers in the "Men's Movement." Robert Bly, Sam Keen, Michael Meade, Mark Gerson and others. While in some sense this was an intentionally gentle response to feminism, at the same time it was an affirmation of the complementary nature of being human—female and male, yin and yang (non-binary wasn't in our thinking). To an extent, the movement was concerned with guys "getting in touch with their feminine side." I could see the value in that, though I wondered if my "good side" was predominantly feminine, or if there was good in being masculine too.

While in seminary we learned (men and women alike) that God could be understood as feminine as well as masculine. Not only is *Elohim*—one name for God in early Genesis—a plural "We" and the Creator formed both male and female in the likeness of the Creator, but the "Presence" of God (*Shekinah*) meeting with Moses in his wilderness tent was feminine, and the Holy Spirit (*Pneuma*) could be a feminine face of the divine. None of this was emphasized, of course, in a predominantly male Christian tradition. Also unsurprising, we didn't hear much about the Goddess in traditions other than Abrahamic religions. Nevertheless, some of us grew comfortable with tweaking the Lord's Prayer to: "Our Mother (or Our Parent) Who art in heaven." Oddly enough, that's still fairly radical, even heretical, in many churches, even some "liberal progressive" ones. Yet, for some of us, this is old news. Of course language needs to be updated, especially with ancient books and theologies written and propagated primarily by men.

Some threads of religious tradition celebrate that human beings, if not the Deity, have elements of both male and female. Mystics seemed to understand that. Moses, Jesus and Paul, not so much. Yet, we can find at least a few places in Hebrew and Christian scriptures where women are esteemed, or in some "spiritualized" sense, equal to men (Queen Esther; Genesis: female and male both created in God's image; Galatians: "In Christ there is neither male nor female"). However, women were rarely in leadership, and certainly not writing scriptures.

In boyhood, male friends, cousins and I were completely consumed by play-acting as warriors, soldiers and he-men. We would slay all enemies, claiming victories over dinosaurs, Nazis and any other evil bad-guys. Protecting defenseless girls felt natural and "manly". The "damsel in distress" motif seemed to permeate almost all of the shows we watched and books we read. Cringeworthy now, the worst thing we could call a boy was "wuss" or "woman."

When I became a teenage crusader for The Man of Galilee, a muscular Christ with a swagger like John Wayne, I proudly joined the Army of Salvation fighting alongside other gladiators for God and soldiers wielding the "sword of the Spirit." As defenders of the gospel, we put on "the full armor of God" to fight the civil war of faith beside our Commander-in-Chief, Jesus. None of us ever asked why the battle between Good and Evil, God and Satan, never ended. And we neglected to ask why God, and Jesus, needed us to fight for them. Couldn't they fight their own wars?

As we got older we were expected to be "Men of God," strong and faithful protectors of women, children and American Christianity (though this was never said aloud). Jesus was our brother-in-arms, our model for true manhood—tough, yet loving, powerful, yet willing to sacrifice his life for others. No wonder God became a man not a woman!

In her urgent and timely book, *Jesus and John Wayne: How White Evangelicals Corrupted a Faith and Fractured a Nation*, Kristin Kobes Du Mez, professor of history at Calvin University, writes that strong male figures like John Wayne became popular icons of rugged manhood. Though he never actually fought in a war, Wayne "would come to symbolize ... a nostalgic yearning for a mythical 'Christian America, 'a return to 'traditional 'gender roles, and the reassertion of (white) patriarchal authority." As she explains: "Like Wayne, the heroes who best embodied militant Christian masculinity were those unencumbered by traditional Christian virtues. In this way, militant masculinity linked religious and secular conservatism, helping to secure an alliance with profound political ramifications." For many believers, "these militant heroes would come to define not only Christian manhood but Christianity itself." Heroes matter.

I wonder, do we hear so much about "values" because, like Wayne, the "virtues" are seen as too weak or "feminine"? Kristin Kobes Du Mez minces no words when she calls this a "cult of masculinity." She concludes her timely book with a challenge. To understand the tears in the fabric of our communities, "[we need to appreciate] how this ideology developed," take it seriously, and resist it forcefully in order to dismantle it.

17

Journey to the Forest of Freethought: A Secular Parable

(originally published on *Friendly Freethinker*)

My roots are in the Pacific Northwest, specifically Western Washington. Growing up in the soggy suburbs of Seattle, I soaked in the natural environment as it absorbed me. Early on I began to look up. Storm clouds, birds, planes (my father worked at Boeing) and my beloved trees. As a young boy, the trees in our yard and the surrounding woods, constantly beckoned. My first "calling" was to explore both out and up. Climbing trees was not just second nature, it was first. Helping my Dad build a small platform on low branches, what we called a "tree fort," set me on my earliest "mission"—to scamper up cedars, pines, firs, alders. A vertical adventure, ascending the green canopy where I was alone and could see a new world, from a higher perspective, without being seen.

Still in childhood, *a new tree was shown to me*. An odd thing. No species I could identify. A tree with no roots or branches, no leaves or fruit. A dead tree, naked, rugged with no bark. I was told it was used for execution in the Roman Empire long ago. This one tree—called "Cross"—was not for climbing, not for tree houses. It was used to kill a kindly, bearded, be-robed young man named Jesus. We had to imagine him on the tree since we were Protestants. The emphasis was on resurrection. The young teacher had come back to life. Strangely enough, the empty tree hung as a symbol, in the church, around my neck—a message that "he's alive" yet "he died for me." A very sad thought I felt guilty about, though I was told "he took my guilt." I was forgiven, but could never forgive myself that something I did—as a child!—caused him to die such a horrible death. I would have liked to climb a tree with him, but now that one tree only made me think of blood, suffering and death. I cried for him, and for myself.

Then I began to branch out in my experience. I learned that this tree was in a whole forest of trees, a forest of the Christian faith: Protestant, Catholic, Orthodox, Evangelical, Pentecostal and more. This was a thick "ecumenical" grove. Each towering tree of tradition was decorated in many ways by those groups, carved in creeds and confessions, but the message was similar: *the Cross is the most important tree.*

My roots were still deep in that forest when I discovered there were other forests with other trees that grew beyond the Christian forest. In my evangelical college, I heard wondrous stories of different faiths and read interesting scriptures made from species I had never heard of. Most importantly, I met people who lived by those stories and scriptures just as I lived by mine, whose trees were not dead, whose branches were never scarred with bloody iron nails. These new forests were actually very old. I had just never been told about them. I was surprised to find wisdom in each forest, browsing among trees new to me, yet somehow familiar. Others were seeking roots too, simply looking for ways to grow and thrive. And each cherished their own forest, clinging to their own trees, as I did my own cold, rigid, splintered tree.

After studying to be a minister of The One Tree, I was drawn to a new kind of forest, one where a diverse variety of species were growing side by side, nourished by the same soil, sun and rain. I found a sense of home in this "interfaith" landscape where one tree did not dominate but all trees were respected and cared for, even as people lived, learned and enjoyed livelihood together. That delightful forest provided sustenance, shade and shelter to many wanderers, outsiders who did not identify with any specific kind of tree. The human species mattered more than any species of tree, especially the artificial variety.

As years passed, I emerged from that forest of faiths and another terrain of thought presented itself. I worked on a farm and cleared paths through thick forests on a salty-sea island. Calling myself a "pathfinder," I practiced a daily mindfulness of how I was impacting the land—planting, harvesting and consuming vegetables—and how the land was impacting me. I kept climbing (in body and mind) and found the best cell reception was high in a cedar! It was easy to imagine I was immersed in "The Spirit of Nature," a part of everything; I became a pantheistic, pagan sort of student of all my fellow inhabitants on that wild patch of earth. I listened, observed, reflected and wrote, trying to put into words, on more paper cut from living trees, a new sense of Life and Living.

With a fresh harvest of ideas, leaving paths in places no one had walked, I left that forest, journeyed from that land, carrying a lighter pack full of curiosity. *Faith had faded into the forests, washed away by the rains of reason.* I still climb (on my Christmas birthday, if I can). Now, I simply see trees grounded in dark and dusty earth. Living, life-giving trees are enough. No dead and denuded tree can stand as a symbol of health and hope. No forest can stand for all other forests. Now I see the trees, and the forest—one vast forest of many species, each a home, giving life to those who live in and near, and each providing the breath of life to us all.

No forest is better than another. No species of tree is more valuable. No individual tree is more magnificent than any other (though one aged juniper near Tahoe, a giant sequoia in the Sierra and a tall fir near the Pacific Coast make me wonder!). I emerged from the forests of faith and that has made all the difference. I wouldn't want them cut down for "holy places," scriptures, or out of hatred for faith itself. When healthy trees are preserved, not used as weapons or symbols of death (or other worlds beyond death), when tended for the benefit of all, forests of freethought may find root, planting new sprouts, sending refreshing green life to a thirsty world.

If old or new groves stand as invitations for new generations to climb, to delight in new perspectives, who knows what they will see up there, ascending into wonder.

18

The Pleasure of Discovering You Are Wrong

The writer Norman Maclean, son of a Presbyterian minister, author of the book, *A River Runs Through It* (made into a film directed by Robert Redford), was born in Iowa and grew up in Missoula, Montana. He worked for the U.S. Forest Service and then became a professor of English at the University of Chicago. He died in 1990, just before another book was published, *Young Men and Fire*.

Maclean was fascinated, perhaps haunted, by the tragic deaths of 13 Smokejumpers who died in August 1949 fighting a fire near the Missouri River in Montana. These young men parachuted into a narrow canyon—Mann Gulch—and were caught in a fast-moving firestorm. As they tried in vain to outrun the fire on a steep slope, three made it over a ridge to safety, several others survived for a short time, and the rest fell before the power of the flames.

In *Young Men and Fire*, Maclean tells the story of what happened that terrible day, tracing the historical record, speaking with the survivors, and hiking into that burned over ground. The storytelling compels the reader to keep searching, continue investigating with a curiosity for the truth. As he sees it, the official reports were written too fast and there were too many unanswered questions about what the Smokejumpers really did, why they were trapped, what the actual conditions were and why only a few survived. It's a real mystery story.

In Maclean's intriguing narrative, I picked up the trail of one fire behavior scientist he refers to, Harry Gisborne. Gisborne had theories about the cause of the Mann Gulch "blowup"—the explosive wall of flame. In Maclean's words: "He was to discover in Mann Gulch on the last day of his life that both his theories were wrong." Gisborne was a competent researcher so "to his credit, he was the first one to point out his error and was happily preparing to wake up the next day to correct his theories … ."

Gisborne didn't die from the fire, or any fire. He died of a coronary while studying that mountain canyon to see if his views of the fire were accurate. Once again, Maclean: "This is the death of a scientist, a scientist who did much to establish a science. On the day of his death he had the pleasure of discovering that his theory … was wrong … . For a scientist, this is a good way to live and die, maybe the ideal way for any of us—excitedly finding we were wrong and excitedly waiting for tomorrow to come so we can start over." For a time, in his own search for truth, Maclean followed Gisborne, then found other trails, other theories to follow.

What lessons are found on the fiery paths of faith, or in our own search for sparks of truth? We are dropped into unknown lands (ancient Palestine, India, Arabia, China) and immediately face decisions, even dangerous choices. If we choose an alternative trail, or mountain, could we lose our family, community, sanity (or fear we might)? The fires we face, or run from, might kill us, or prove to be brighter insights for new paths forward. Will we survive if we no longer believe the literal truth of scriptures, or the "divine authority" of clergy or creeds? Are there dangerous ideas to contemplate? Is it worth challenging those who warn us away from healthier, more liberating viewpoints?

Later in his extended analysis of what happened that fateful day in Mann Gulch, Maclean wrote: "Coming to recognize you are wrong is like coming to recognize you are sick. You feel bad long before you admit you have any of the symptoms and certainly long before you are willing to take your medicine." A wise observation. Many times along the way, Maclean had to admit he was on the wrong track, maybe close to being accurate, but a correction in direction was necessary. This is of course good science, not religion. Yet why not religion—good and better religion?

Can religious faith handle the fires of freethought, the swirling questions that chase those who try to break free of restrictive environments? If you are a person of faith, how do you measure the risk? Most importantly, at least in my way of thinking, what do you do when your theories, beliefs, opinions about matters of faith, are wrong, or at least inadequate to life's challenging situations? Is there a clear path of escape, a way to freedom?

If you are a secular person, are you able to face the fires of failed theories? Can you find pleasure, a kind of deeply felt satisfaction, discovering you may be wrong?

Maclean's observations offer lasting lessons to illuminate our imaginations.

19

The New American Religion of Nature

(from a presentation at Sunday Assembly,

Berkeley, California, 2016)

"Bathed in such beauty, watching the expressions ever varying on the faces of the mountains, watching the stars, which here have a glory that the lowlander never dreams of, watching the circling seasons, listening to the songs of the waters and winds and birds, would be endless pleasure. And what glorious cloudlands I should see, storms and calms—a new heaven and a new earth every day, aye and new inhabitants."
("Secular Scripture" from John Muir,
My First Summer in the Sierra)

I bumped into old Johnny Muir on a Sierra mountain trail about 25 years ago. Reading his Journals and his first book, *The Mountains of California*, I sensed he was sauntering right along with me in the highcountry air. Walking along with the energetic Scotsman, I came to see him as more than a wild naturalist, founder of national parks and clubs. I came to see him as a prophet kind of fellow—like some new kind of secular chaplain— a heretical wanderer and wonderer whose chapel was wide open and wild Nature.

Many people know the basic story of Muir, that he was born in Dunbar, Scotland in 1838. . .178 years ago this

April 21st. Some may know that he lived for years near the San Francisco Bay, with his wife and 2 daughters. He collected flowers and redwood fronds on Mount Tamalpais and across Point Reyes, where I've been wandering for over 35 years.

You've probably heard that Muir was raised in strict religion...the Bible was the Family Book. Thankfully, he broke free and bounded up higher trails—found other books, other scriptures—along trails higher than any heaven. Actually he hiked right into heaven. Yosemite was his Holy of Holies.

Muir left us way more than books, parks and clubs. He left us a challenge that I'm not sure we've even noticed...and maybe we're not yet ready for it—even after 100 years.

A few years ago I gave a sermon at a local church and called upon the wisdom of John Muir and his side kick John Burroughs—the freethinking NY Naturalist. My sermon was titled, "God is Green" and my point was that, at least for me, any sense of God has been soaked in and absorbed by Nature. Nature is the only God for me. So, finally, there is only Nature...only Nature.

I've been reading Jay Wexler's book, *When God Isn't Green*. Wexler is a professor of Law at Boston University who teaches environmental law and church/state issues.

Wexler is a Bill Bryson-type, jaunting around the world to see what effect religious practice and ritual have on the environment. I'd like to imagine John Muir joining him for this journey. Observing Taoists burning joss paper in Singapore, filling the air with toxic smoke. Hindus dumping hundreds of statues of Ganesh in the Ganges. Native

Americans "taking" eagles for their feathers. Jews in Israel lighting huge bonfires for a minor holiday, that makes the whole country smell like smoke. He goes to Guatemala to see farmers hacking down forests of palm trees for Christians to celebrate Palm Sunday. Buddhists in Taiwan "mercy releasing" thousands of turtles and birds, only to capture them again to make money for temples. Then there's the mountain of plastic water bottles left by Muslim pilgrims on the Hajj to Mecca.

Wexler isn't anti-religious at all, yet he points out that "religious pilgrimages cause significant environmental damage" year after year. He also notes that religious people seem to really like to Burn things...lots of things.

This connects with what I wrote in *Life After Faith* (republished as *From Faith to Freethought*) about cutting down whole forests of trees for churches and crosses and the paper for millions upon millions of bibles—add to this the millions of qur'ans, vedas, sutras, torahs and libraries jammed full of theological books. Pretty disappointing to see the effect that faith can have on the world's environment.

But Wexler is hopeful...and so am I. And at least some of my hopefulness has come from John Muir kicking me in the seat, out into the fresh air where theology and religion don't really matter much at all.

Muir still leads us into the wilds. Wild land, wild forests, wild mountains...a wild wilderness of ideas. This is where Freethinkers are born and thrive!

Speaking of freethought, I have a theory. It's Heretical and Apostate and Infidel and Blasphemous—in a nice way!

Here's my reasoning: America has sprouted a lot of Religion. Spirituality can be picked up and rinsed off in the farmers 'markets of faith all across the land. It's a harvest planted in the compost of the continent.

But my theory is that there is *One American Religion* (or call it a Spirituality or simply an Experience, if you wish) greater than all the rest. Millions of people flock and herd to this New Religion every year. It has more temples and sacred places than any other. It has the most inspiring Holy Book of them all. And, honestly speaking, it can boast of the Greatest God above and beyond any and all Gods ever invented by wild-fearing humans.

And here's the surprising thing: this New Faith that is really beyond any Faith—it's not even noticed by most people! Unrecognized. It stares us right in the face but we don't see it. Very few even know that they're Members!

Have you figured it out by now? Are you getting the picture? This is radical stuff. Literally: Back to the Roots radical.

The New American Religion was practiced by John Muir, John Burroughs, Thoreau and many more of their fellow saunterers. Those wild thinkers were among the Founders of this Faith—this faith above faiths... or under and below, all faiths. In the ground beneath all faiths. The forgotten ground beneath all this stuff we call spiritual religion.

Who can teach us about this New American Experience? Who are the clergy, the chaplains, the priests and rabbis, imams and gurus of this religion? Are you ready for it? Can you hear it? *The National Park Service!* One hundred years ago, just after Muir died, the National Park Service was born. You could say Muir was resurrected—into thousands of rangers and interpreters and educators! Park Service people are the clergy, the caretakers, of a vast system of 400 sites across the nation. 84 million acres. 59 National Parks. 300 million people visit each year. 300 million of the faithful...the New Faithful at Old Faithful, who don't even know they're in Church...in the Temple!

SEE...that's one damn huge Religion!

Ok, let's be clear: Like Muir, we have to take these old words out of our mental backpacks and look at them in the light of the campfire—the campfire of our Reason: this is a Religion without Religion. A Faith without Faith. A Spirituality without Spirit. Nothing SUPER-natural about it. It's SUPER enough just as it is. And...really...we may have to let go of ALL these old words, because we live in a New World...a New Wild World of Wonder. That's it! That's our WOW...the new form of AMEN! *WOW—World of Wonder*. Those old words maybe just don't work anymore. W-WOW!

What does the **Secular Sanctuary of Nature** look like? How do we identify this radical Religionless Religion?

We need a new perspective to see this and begin to understand. When I lived in my one room cabin on an island in Washington, I had to climb 50 feet up an old Cedar to get cell reception. I called it my Phone Tree. People couldn't believe I was calling them swaying at the top of a tree. The birds and squirrels couldn't believe it either!

Well, it gave me a different perspective on connecting, on relationships that might look different than anything we've ever seen, anything we've ever *thought* of.

Thankfully we have people like Saint Johnny to help ...

Preachers of the *Gospel of Nature*.
Chaplains like Thoreau, Burroughs, Ed Abbey, Rachel Carson, Wilma Dykeman, Gretel Erhlich and Janine Benyus.
Poets like Whitman, Mary Oliver, Maya Angelou and many more.
Choirs like the waterfalls and birdcalls, the frogs, whales and wolves.
Scriptures written by natural laws, by evolution, by glaciers, by earthquakes and tornadoes and tsunamis, disease and death (what? you thought it's just about the happy stuff?).

It's not really a new religion, you see. Thomas Paine preached it way back in the 1790's. Ingersoll preached it all over America. Now, Ken Burns preaches it. What's the message of this wild experience? Don't ask ME. Ask the scientists, the explorers—ask the bison, the beetle and the bird —search for it in your own brain.

So, Muir left a simple message, a revolutionary message, a simple "gospel" still echoing in the sanctuaries across the country, across the planet. A gritty gospel of good news...but positive, compassionate and relevant...

Muir Proclaims: Go! Get Thyself OUT! Go out! Go out there, into the wild places (even in your backyard, your garden, your neighborhood). Saunter, passed your fear...saunter without destination. Listen. Learn. Leave the screens, leave the dreams of other worlds. Turn THIS CELL off (the mental distractions). Get TEXTED by Nature. Get TWEETED by Wonder. Get EMAILED by the excitement of Exploration. Leave your spirituality, your desperate need to connect with something or someone beyond the beauty. Leave the Spirit and catch the Spirit of Secularism. As Muir tells us, *Beauty is All*—Everything—the only God left and worth respecting...the God beyond all Gods. Be a student, be a chaplain, be a lover of it all.

This is a practice of *Sacred Secularity*.

Welcome to John Muir's Sanctuary!

And NOW...Let us lift up our heads, open our eyes wide, and set free the cosmos in our craniums, for a **Secular Prayer:**

"Nature, Ahhh. Nature. You don't hear us. You don't care. You aren't interested in Prayer, or Worship—or that we want you to Look and Think like Us. You aren't a Person to talk to at all. But oh, you're Amazing, Nature. Full of Beauty. You ARE Beauty. Full of Wonder. So are We. Here we are, silly seculars, talking to ourselves.

Oh, and John—John Muir—you can't hear us either, but we hear you. Your voice is still calling to us from across a century, out in the wilderness. Our secular evangelist, reminding us, because we need reminding again and again, to be open to the WOW experience. Pure secular, marvelous, amazing, INcredible, earthy. Thank you, Johnny boy.

What a Wild World of Wonder we have to explore and celebrate."

And the people said,

WOW!... WOW!... WOW!

20

Freethought, Faith and the Future

(could the secular vision of *Star Trek* offer a way forward?)

This essay was submitted to the "Response" magazine published by Seattle Pacific University, the wealthy west coast evangelical university where I received my B.A. in Religion and Philosophy. After a month and two emails, the editor tersely responded that "it's not a good fit for us." Yet, as you'll see, this was carefully written (with a touch of humor) as an invitation to consider what the future could look like if our various cultures of belief chose to cooperate, as Star Trek *often envisions. The college is proud to proclaim they are "engaging the culture" yet, like many evangelicals, they don't offer much of a "response" to the rest of us–they merely mean to proudly preach their version of the gospel, having little to learn from frightening alien species like me. Disappointing. But not unexpected.*

I have been a *Star Trek* fan since the original series. Gene Roddenberry's vision of space exploration transported my imagination all the way through *Next Generation*, *Deep Space Nine*, *Voyager*, *Enterprise* and beyond. *Star Trek: Discovery* has a few good characters and *Picard* has potential, yet I'm looking ahead to the next frontier ... where no series has gone before.

At its best, Trek presents a hopeful, cooperative vision of the future rather than the endless conflict of the *Star Wars* meme with its emphasis on battles between the "force" and the "dark side."

As I reflect, Trek has been one thread winding like a wormhole through my years of faith, ministry and beyond. It's the "beyond" that I want to speak to here. How can the "beyond" relate to the "before"? Can people with faith honestly relate to the "beyonders"?

This is of particular concern in my life, my teaching and writing, and in our divided world. How can we find "common space" to expand our knowledge out beyond our own, often irrational, fears?

In the *Star Trek* universe, a federation of planets cooperates not to dominate but to investigate other worlds. The crews of starships like Voyager and Enterprise (enterprise: a difficult undertaking or project) are radically diverse in gender, ethnicity, species and religion. With all their differences the crew is committed to a mission to explore, discover, make first contact, build alliances, all of which takes steady effort—a difficult undertaking!

There may be enterprising parallels as we travel through the galaxies of the godly and godless in our day.

It's good to put a face on freethinkers. Brace yourself for my personal trek and trajectory: raised Protestant, "saved" at a Billy Graham revival, active in Baptist and Presbyterian youth groups, sang in church choirs, led Bible studies, prayed through a Pentecostal and "Messianic Jewish" period, Campus Crusade leadership training … conservative Christian college … on through seminary, ordination, ministry, chaplaincy, ecumenical non-profit work, teaching and writing. Gradually, due to a change of course heading, I emerged as a humanist! (see *My Address is a River*).

My four years at Seattle Pacific University were critically important. Born in Seattle and emerging from my faith "bubble" I became immersed in the history of religion, world wisdom traditions and Philosophy. *Confronting the Great Questions challenged my Great Answers.* I took those questions onboard, packed with wonder and curiosity. They became companions on my voyage across the expanse of marginalized ministry.

Through years in interfaith chaplaincy I was called upon to build bridges of relationships every day. These spanned socio-economic, racial and religious divides. It was a special delight to be asked by a jail inmate, a person on the street or a person of a particular faith: "What religion do you represent?" "Is your chaplaincy a Christian ministry?"

The bafflement on faces was obvious when I said things like, "I'm a Christian minister, but this is an interfaith chaplaincy; I represent the compassion of those communities." Over time I grew to see that our work of listening and assisting where needed was more important than spending valuable time discussing opinions about God, though we did that too (when it didn't distract).

In other words, bridge-building was more important (and relevant) than wall-building (and the thickest walls are in our minds).

We all know these are fearful times. Yet, we can't be afraid to engage people who think and believe differently than we do. So let me clear the air and assure believers you can engage people like me and still be ok!

Secular people like me are not out to steal anyone's faith or silence the voices of faith in the public square. We're just inter-

ested in hearing ALL the voices, not only one privileged voice. And theists should be heard, equally with non-theists. We just happen to think our world and our communities are better secular than sectarian.

To be "secular" isn't meant to scare anyone. It merely refers to "this present world and no other." That may cause a believer some shaking, shock or sadness, but don't we have to live side by side in the world now, heaven or no heaven?

Freethinkers like me are not trying to delete religion and download a godless world. We're simply interested in shared software and reasonable dialogue that benefits the whole community rather than one "exceptional" user group. The Freethought tradition (think of Thomas Paine, Elizabeth Cady Stanton, Robert Ingersoll but also "heretics" like Jesus) is fueled not by strict atheism but a healthy agnosticism. Essentially, freethinkers question the authority of orthodoxy (those who claim they hold the "right opinions"). They remind us that humility is foundational for spirituality as well as skepticism. As I learned in my first college Philosophy class, Socrates was the wisest of all, because he could say "I know that I don't know" (compare Jesus 'silence when asked, "What is truth?").

Humanists like me are neither without ethics nor ignoring the wisdom contained in sacred scriptures or spiritual traditions. *We simply search for wisdom wherever it may be found.* Rather than seeking guidance outside of the natural world, human reason and the human heart are the sources of good or bad decisions. As some humanists say, we can be "good without god."

And just because we left our supernatural beliefs along the journey doesn't mean we want everyone to abandon their cherished devotion. After leaving the church, my ordination and my faith, I chose to stay in relationship with people I cared about. There are believers in my family, among my closest friends and my wife is a Christian minister. My classes, weekly columns and published books welcome engagement from freethinkers with or without faith.

Given my relationships, if and when I hear an atheist angrily attack someone's religious beliefs, I often speak up and push back. I've been known to defend sensible religion (nonsense is another matter). All seculars shouldn't be judged by unreasonable nonbelievers any more than believers judged by the fanatics.

To Go Where We've Never Been Before

Creating opportunities to bring the faithful and faithless together for respectful bridge-building isn't easy. In fact, it may be a very turbulent "enterprise." But it's wonderful to see! And I often ask: What's the alternative to collaboration? Do we need more barriers and fences between people who label themselves in various ways? Do we really believe everyone should think and believe just like we do? Do we always have to be doing battle with the "dark side" or can we "beam down" to something more positive, creative and constructive?

A regular theme that runs through many *Star Trek* episodes is distrust between species encountered world by world. An innate fearfulness greets the crew in every new interaction. But the attempt is worth it, to push beyond the fears, switch on the universal translator, and take a chance that communication can happen—and maybe a new alliance.

How about we try this back here on earth? This doesn't

need to be a threat pushing us back into defensive positions. Those who believe in other worlds and those who are skeptical can land somewhere, because we're already here (and the same species!). This tiny blue planet is already our common home, whether or not we choose to think there is another, better home out there.

Neil deGrasse Tyson, director of the Hayden Planetarium, may be infamous in some religious circles because he sees no evidence for a Good God in the universe. On the other hand, he refrains from calling himself an atheist. He's not anti-religious, trying to use phasers or photons to evaporate the world of belief. With an active agnosticism he's inviting us to think, and be amazed, together.

Astronomer Carl Sagan, who thought skeptical science and sacred spirituality could co-exist, once said, "Imagination will often carry us to worlds that never were. But without it we go nowhere."

I'm not sure about you, but I'm honored to join a crew that celebrates imagination and includes diverse viewpoints. In fact, I'm uncomfortable if the room is full of people who only think like me. I don't just want to hear myself; I want to know what you think.

So, let's gather on the bridge, take the helm, engage and explore without fear, shall we? There's a whole universe open out there!

21

Tom Paine's Church

A Mindful Reflection on Mindlessness

"My own mind is my own church."
~Thomas Paine, *The Age of Reason* (1794)

Breathe. Step. Smile. Breathe. Years of mindfully meditative walks at a favorite Zen retreat and farm on the California coast taught me to breathe (at least to be more aware of breathing) but also to let go of meditation itself. It's Zen; it's not meant to "make sense" (be completely rational). But a Zen practice is intended to cause a bit of head-shaking faced with contradictions. "Let it go—don't be attached," even if it means releasing our hold on an instruction to "Let it go—don't be attached."

Shaking your head is a valuable lesson in itself. "Be aware; don't hold so tight to your head—your mind." I'd like to be attached to my head, but I get the point.

During those silent walks, drawing waves of salty sea air deep into my lungs, I was devoting long hours to anxious thinking about fatherhood, chaplaincy, the unmindful messes of my life and the lives of so many. Breathe. Step. Smile. I learned to be skeptical of being "in my head" too much as well as not being too caught up in other people's heads, and lives. The alert practice of contemplating breath and steps opened a wider awareness and appreciation for nature and the nature of my mind even while being mindful of others.

In the midst of daily stressful distractions demanding attention from every direction, the letting go, the release, was liberating, and I think the practice made me a better thinker as well.

Mind your mindfulness while you learn to be mindless. This could be a partial summary of what I have learned from Buddhism. The Awakened One ("the Buddha") and the traditions of his followers provide us with a delightfully disorienting path for living that consistently insists we leave the path—let it go too.

We need to practice an awakened mindfulness, while having "less mind"—less stuck on our own thinking (beliefs, opinions). Zen welcomes serious thought. It is not "anti-mind." But breathing moments of mindlessness can enhance the pathway too, within reason.

"Within reason" makes the difference. And here's where a closer consideration of Thomas Paine's "meditation" on reason and religion could offer a trail map not only for secular folks (secular: this present breathing world) but those on any path of faith.

I've often mulled over the quotation at the head of this essay (mulling is a kind of freethinker's meditation). "My own mind is my own church" was penned by the flabbergastingly forgotten founder, Thomas Paine (1737-1809) in the opening paragraphs of *The Age of Reason* (1794). He was sharpening the blade he would use on his axe-swinging saunter through the forest of faith (his image, not mine). His aging reason was seasoned by years of reflection on the role of religion in personal and political governance.

In reference to Paine's concise statement, I have frequently placed emphasis on the latter half of the phrase: "my own church." Now I wonder if the emphasis in this famous phrase should swing back to "my own mind." In our day it seems dangerous to let "never mind" be our motto—"Never mind too much thinking here." A wise response to the "neverminders" might better be: "Think about what you're saying, doing, believing." This may provide a more cogent hint at Paine's precise meaning of "church."

We live in a time when a distrust of the reasoning mind and critical thinking can lead to extremes. An almost proud ignorance threatens education, healthcare, science and the environment. Loud voices demand "religious freedom" (for their own religion) or proclaim nonsense that would "Make America Dumb Again." We may do well to heed the call to return to "Tom's Church."

In the arena of religious faith Paine's principle could get twisted and re-written as: "My own heart is my own church." A more popularized focus on "intuition and emotion." How we "feel" about the world takes precedence over how we "think" about our world. Are we stuck with the dichotomy? No, and yes.

To frame these matters around one's "own heart" may be more palatable and preachable to progressive believers as well as more mystically-inclined folks, but the dilemma isn't so easily dismissed. It's not that a "matter of the heart" is necessarily in conflict with a "matter of the mind" (and this is not a matter of mind over matter). The issue, as I see it, relates to who manages the sanctuary—reason or faith. I don't think (or feel) that both can equally handle the task.

Why did Paine write that his mind, rather than his heart or body, "soul" or "spirit," is a sanctuary?

Oddly enough, there may be a flicker of illumination found in this pericope from ancient Buddhist scripture (The *Dhammapada*, sayings of The-Wide-Awake-and-maybe-Woke-One—Buddha):

"Those driven by fear go to many a refuge [sanctuary], to mountains, to forests, to sacred trees and shrines. That, truly, is not a safe refuge, that is not the best refuge." Those who have a basic grasp of Buddhism can anticipate where this is leading: "But the one who takes refuge in the Buddha, the Teachings and the Community" sees with clear wisdom to walk the path through the suffering of life.

"Those driven by fear go to many a refuge." A fine example of freethought as a thorn in the side of spiritualized faith. Seeking the shelter of sanctuary because of a reticence to trust the rational or out of fearful protectiveness may cause us to be less discriminating where we flee—physically and mentally.

It would be a wild leap to claim that Paine found refuge (church, sanctuary) in Buddha and his philosophical path. But, let's leap!

As understood by some Buddhists, definitions are slippery, so we could re-state the saying thusly: Take refuge (find a non-fear-based sanctuary) in the Buddha (the enlightened, awakened mind), the Teachings (wisdom past and present) and Community (the congregation of all living things with their diverse voices).

To awaken is to enlighten and wisely choose freedom

alongside others who are intellectually awakening (consider Paine's own Age of Enlightenment). For guidance, old maps may provide hints (general directions) but it is our responsibility to discover up-to-date maps or, better yet, write our own, based on our own explorations and investigations.

For Paine, the only sacred text to study was the "scripture of creation." Like Muir, Thoreau, Darwin and other naturalists, he saw that the wilderness is only an open classroom to the open mind.

This wild leap to connect philosophies might serve to assist our deeper appreciation for Paine's insights as well as his far-sighted critique of reasonless religion (indeed he urged a "revolution in the system of religion"). This could be a great benefit for people of faith to "clean up the sanctuary" and for secular people to resurrect Paine as an educator and bridge-builder (he once designed a brand new kind of iron bridge— why not design some innovative spans for our day?).

Maybe the leap is simply a conscious step onto a bridge we have built?

Crossing these spans, making these connections, we could gain a Paine-ful perspective (not a pain-less prospect). Letting go of those old maps with their distorted worldviews will lead to a feeling of being lost for some. Yet, as stated, there remain valuable lessons in some texts that span the centuries.

A startling passage from another ancient scripture, the *Upanishads* of Hinduism (III, 9, 1), presents a further context for a leaping Paine:

One sage asks another, "How many gods are there?" "Thousands," is the response.
"Yes, but how many gods are there?"
"Thirty-three." (that's a lot of divine demotions)
The Q and A continues to six, three, two, and my favorite: "One and a half." Finally the teacher presses his colleague, "Yes, but just how many gods are there?"
"One."
Ah, now he's got him.
"Which is the one god?"
We might imagine a long pause and deep sigh.
"Breath," the man says (another name for Brahman, the Creator)

"Amen!," congregants in Tom's Church might shout. This draws us back to a very natural, human experience. A supernatural beyond? Perhaps. But maybe all we have are questions to breath—and the breath is spirit enough, God enough.

I'm not claiming to summarize two historic religions here, yet as a freethinker Paine was responding to any and all orthodoxies (with government or god) that resist or refuse to carry out the necessary questions (to pause, breathe and think) to their logical—or illogical—conclusions. And since "conclusions" can be slick and squishy sometimes (leaping from our hands), this is especially true in matters of belief.

Paine may not have read a *Dhammapada* or *Upanishad* but his reasoning dug down deep into the "heart" of all faiths where that leans toward heart (intuitive feeling) rather than head (rational skepticism).

Many in faith communities nod their heads (ironically)

when the focus is on heart. Yes, they say, it's about the heart and "soul," not so much the head, reason, the brain. These folks aren't always being irrational or anti-rational but there is a fundamental distrust of the brain. They fear that too much reliance on the brain can strain or drain spirituality.

It may be good to remind the mindful that Thomas Paine was a Deist with a Quaker background—believing in a Creator who cannot be known or experienced except through "the creation" including the "inner light" of the human mind. What a person "feels" or imagines (gives an image or face to) concerning the Deistic deity must be checked and balanced by an enlightened (actively awakened) mind.

Are there "mysteries of the unknown" for Paine? Certainly. However, what may appear mysterious is only currently unknown, not necessarily unknowable. Nothing is beyond investigation. And just because we don't understand something we have no need to call strangeness "miracle" requiring either faith or revelation (revelation is mere hearsay in the gospel according to Paine—revealed to thee but not to me).

Appropriate questions remain. Doesn't Paine's sanctuary of the mind simply open the door to making a god of Reason? Isn't this just the old personalistic path to complete relativism?

As for relativism, an individual is about as relative as you can get. We share feelings all the time. Sharing coherent thoughts and ideas takes a further level of ability, we could even say sensibility (as in common sense, dear to the hearty mind of Paine).

Was Paine suggesting he could claim, "God spoke to me in the church of my mind, therefore you must believe"? Not at all. His meaning is fairly clear throughout his writings on human rights and freedom for the whole person. He was consistently mindful of the bigger picture that would include all animated minds. In other words—and this is what sets him apart from any religious truth-claims with their self-proclaimed prophets—Paine stands with the authority of his own mind-church, while defending the right of each person to do the same. There are as many sanctuaries as there are minds.

Placed in a greater context, we could say that the revolutionary Paine was deeply interested in a community of minds. If he was "all in his head" and unmindful to boot, there may never have been a cooperative community of minds to incarnate an Idea called America.

Could reason (the investigations of the intellect) ever be a god? Well, how many gods are there?, asks the sage. Some might deify the mind, but to what purpose? Jesus himself urged his followers to "love God with the mind" as well as the heart, soul and strength. Was he suggesting the mind is divine? Maybe. But perhaps more a tool or trail in the direction of the divine (ineffable immensity), and that somehow choosing to use that tool or trail was a form of devotion. That could be taken "by faith," or the devoted might accept the challenge to take it "by serious thought."

Paine might agree with Jesus (he had great respect for him as a human being)—with qualifications. If we can know anything about a god it must be through a direct experience with the observable world, presented with verifiable evidence to reasoning minds. Anything else, any other statement about a God-experience, needs to be fully open to question and critique, though not necessarily respect, unless respectful of reason itself.

Serious thought, linked to a meaningful practice of mindfulness, must be interested in truth and pragmatic results —take for instance a Revolution to create a new nation. Could that "idea" be more truthfully pragmatic? Anything less true, real or practical is essentially nonsense, and the nonsensical (unreasonable) is such even if dressed up in "holy" writings, robes, rituals or the religions themselves.

Naturalist John Burroughs seemed to be walking on the muddy path with Paine, sauntering reverently into the sanctuary, when he wrote:

"If we do not go to church so much as did our [parents], we go to the woods much more, and are much more inclined to make a temple of them than they were" ("The Gospel of Nature," *Time and Change*, 1912). The gospel of Burroughs, like the gospel of Paine, offered good news of churches and temples (mosques and synagogues) waiting to be discovered. These are not "made holy" by any source or authority. They are natural sanctuaries free and welcoming to any and all.

The power of Paine-ful thinking is that we can always turn to the backdrop—the common sense that set fire to the American Revolution. The irresistible energy of free persons with free minds and a courageous common sense claiming their rights, set the foundation for a mindful analysis of the beliefs that would divide and conquer the will and subjugate reason . Paine's dangerous but essential wild leap was one of joy— though he wrote most of *The Age of Reason* in a Parisian prison—because the Revolution was not only about declarations and documents, it was a life and death liberation "fought for thought"—heady ideas that changed the real world—this present, secular world.

His own mind was his sanctuary, his own country was the world and "to do good was [his] religion." Always stretching the boundaries and crossing the borders, Thomas Paine left us a secular legacy that not only leaves wide open space for freedom of beliefs, ideas, questions and the deepest feelings of the heart, but wild lands for exploration across the unknown, perhaps unlimited, sanctuaries of the mind.

Paine's personal practice seems both meditative and reasonable. Breathe. Step. Smile. Breathe. Think. Act. Breathe … .

22

When Science Becomes "Spirituality"

(first posted on the *Secular Chaplain* blog)

You can be the most brilliant philosopher or scientist in the world, but it's still easy to fall into childlike thinking. We default to "spiritual" or religious language because it's the only language we've ever been taught to describe these feelings.

Reading the account of one physicist (Alan Lightman, https://www.pbs.org/newshour/show/a-scientist-stares-into-infinity-and-finds-space-for-spirituality) who had an experience of...well, I'll let him tell it:

"One summer night, I was out in the ocean in a small boat. It was a dark, clear night, and the sky vibrated with stars. I laid down in the boat and looked up. After a few minutes, I found myself falling into infinity. I lost all track of myself, and the vast expanse of time extending from the far distant past to the far distant future seemed compressed to a dot. I felt connected to something eternal and ethereal, something beyond the material world."

He goes on to say you can't prove or disprove this is a God-experience. He's right.

"[You] can't use scientific arguments to analyze or understand the feeling I had that summer night when I lay down in the boat and looked up and felt part of something far larger than myself. I'm still a scientist. I still believe that the world is made

of atoms and molecules and nothing more. But I also believe in the power and validity of the spiritual experience."

He says we may think the universe is only physical, material, yet "We also long for the permanent, some grand and eternal unity."

I wonder why he can't simply say, "I had a feeling. It was a wonderful feeling," and leave it at that? Did he somehow, someway, "fall into infinity"? Was he "connected"? Was he "a part of something larger"?

This is what happens when we have a feeling and we *have* to describe it as more than a feeling. It *has* to be "spiritual"; it *has* to be about "God" (in whatever cultural or imaginative framework we imagine Her/Him/It).

I understand the feeling. I just wonder why we choose one default, one language we feel we have to use to talk about our feelings.

. . .

I once jotted down these words: "A secular chaplain, like the Constitution, tips the hat to religion (with due respect), but never bends the knee (with reverence)."

There may or may not be a connection with the physicist's story.

23

Walls of Mirrors, Windows or Sliding Doors

(from a letter to Rob Boston, editor of *Church and State*, Americans United for the Separation of Church and State)

As a proud member of *Americans United* I have followed the persistence of their "essential workers" protecting valuable walls that hold democracy together. I have also admired their efforts knocking on other walls that need to fracture and fall. Several personal stories illustrate the dual responsibility we face together.

In 1979, following graduation from college, I backpacked across Europe. Arriving in divided Berlin, I passed through the wall at Checkpoint Charlie into East Berlin. Ten years later, in 1989, I watched tearfully as that wall was brought down by the people on both sides, one hammer blow at a time. Later I read that many in that city continued to sense a wall remained—there was still a "wall in the head."

I carried that image with me through years of interfaith work. As a county jail chaplain for a decade, I regularly passed through walls, steel doors and fences lined with razor wire. As an outsider among insiders I spent many hours "doing time" with women and men locked away, hidden from our eyes, in a world of walls. As a chaplain on the streets for another decade, it became clear as glass: some walls are needed, and roofs as well.

What I've learned through these years full of images and stories is something quite obvious, though easy to miss:

Some walls are necessary, others are not. As Robert Frost poetically reminded us, whenever we build walls we ought to know who is walled out and who is walled in. Not simply which groups are divided, but the individuals, the faces, names and stories we are slicing apart and separating.

Border boundaries between nations make sense, yet, as cellist Pablo Casals purportedly asked: "Love of one's country is a splendid thing, but why should love stop at the border?" One of our freethought heroes, Thomas Paine, famously stated: "My country is the world and my religion is to do good." Taken together, these two quotes call into question the purpose of any artificial divisions across the globe, especially those borders in our brains.

When I reflect on these wise insights, I'm left wondering—maybe all these walls are mirrors. If we only see ourselves then we only act for ourselves. Then, no community is possible, no country can be a Union. However, if the walls were windows maybe something else would happen. Did you see those pictures from the Southern border wall showing children on teeter-totters placed right through the tall steel fence? Maybe that's the image we need; our call to action. A teeter-totter is useless if someone sits on one side but there's no one to balance, to take the risk to join. Yet, we have to sense there are some good people over there and it may turn out we're on the same side, teetering on the edge of something better than barriers.

Having been a religious professional for many years of my life, these images seem particularly apropos to religion. Many religions produce wall-builders, fence-defenders. I used to be one of those. So, if there is a barrier to protect and defend, I want to make sure I'm not tottering between "them" and "us."

When it comes to separation of religion and state, this wall is no game. Sometimes it feels like people are lobbing god-grenades over the wall. That is foolish, fruitless and fundamentally faithless. Mental blocks just build more blockhouses (and blockheads).

When our county wanted to provide funds for a church to create a large mural on a sanctuary wall, I wrote several local leaders to question that. More complained and the funds were not given. Visiting the church, I saw the good work they are doing in our community (without a taxpayer-funded mural). Citizen pushback wasn't persecution of the church, it was protection, a gentle reminder one wall —*The Wall of Separation*— may not have a pretty painting on it, but it does provide something beautiful for *We the People*.

Whenever I write our "representatives" in Washington (the pious politicians I call trumpublicans), the reply is essentially: "Thank you for writing. I'll keep your opinion in mind *when I vote the opposite*." I simply let them know there are constituents like my wife and me who are watching ... and voting.

It can be discouraging, this relentless defense of the Fence of Freedom, but Americans United helps keep a sliding glass door open in my mind. When I feel "stone-walled" by preachers or politicians I look for passageways through the obstructions. I think this is exactly what A.U. does day in and day out. Executive Director, Rachel Laser, Rob Boston, advocates and attorneys are diligently working to transform the mirrors into windows and then hopefully doors. Ultimately, in a free and democratic society—especially one with so many who claim to follow a God Who doesn't choose sides—we can hope people would keep the glass clean for better vision ... eyes to see, ears to hear.

As more diverse voices join in the window-making work of A.U. and partner organizations, I need look no further than my own household for encouragement. My wife Carol often snatches up the latest *Church and State* before I get a chance to read it. As a progressive faith leader, she is as concerned as I am about threats to the "old rugged wall" that separates Religion and Government. She shares my alarm at the rise of Christian Nationalism. We share a common commitment to speak out, to "hold the wall" at any cost.

When we hear misguided believers fervently seeking to put God, Bibles and prayer "back" in schools, we shake our heads in dis-belief, since we don't believe that's right, rational or responsible for Americans. As Berliners know, the "wall in the head" may be the hardest to crack. We all have to stand up to the barriers in the brains, because building them begins in the brain. Can we polish the glass so more can see who is over there, across the border, behind the prison walls?

Americans United inspires those who have seen their reflection to replace the mirrors with clear glass and a sliding door, to really see who's there, and why. We need to be defenders of some walls while simultaneously deconstructing others.

Carol, my clergy spouse, says: "Thank God, for Americans United!" As a secular freethinker, I say: "Thank Good, and Amen!"

24

Sacrament of a Secular Saint

(Published on *Patheos* in 2015)

*"[You ask] When are you coming down [from the mountains]?
Ask the Lord—Lord Sequoia."* ~John Muir

In the college Literature course I teach on "a wild spirituality of nature" we have lively discussions on redefining the sacred, the spiritual, the gods in a more down-to-earth context (where we all have to live together). With freethinkers like John Muir, John Burroughs and their circles, we explore the outer edges of ideas and faith (note: I no longer use the term "spirituality" except to question what it means).

One tradition we have in classes is to read from a selection I hand out to students. I get to lean back against the wall and listen as a chorus of voices—theist and nontheist—read line after line of inspiring Nature writing from a century past. It brings great ideas alive. Truly delightful. Students laugh and sigh, get teary or troubled, which all leads to more good dialogue.

Recently I handed out a playful piece by John Muir—a letter he wrote to his friend and mentor Jeanne Carr in 1870. Muir had just taken up residence in his "temple," his "church"—Yosemite Valley. The exuberant Scotsman thought he would tease, writing from "Squirrelville" with the date of "Nut Time."

"I'm in the woods, woods, woods and they are in me-ee-ee. The King tree and me have sworn eternal love. . .and I've taken the sacrament with Douglass Squirrel, drank Sequoia wine, Sequoia blood, and with its rosy purple drops I am writing this woody gospel letter."

Muir knows he is acting the heretic, pushing the limits with the proper sensibilities of his friend's faith, but he can't resist. He sensed Jeanne could handle it, and manage a smile.

"I wish I was so drunk and Sequoical that I could preach the green brown woods to all the juiceless world, descending from this divine wilderness like a John Baptist eating Douglass Squirrels and wild honey or wild anything, crying, Repent for the Kingdom of Sequoia is at hand."

Later, a last poke at his brilliant but more socially respectable, friend:

"Would that some of you wise—terribly wise social scientists might discover some method of living as true to nature as. . .the 'master spirit of the tree tops'[the squirrel]. . ."

By the way, Jeanne Carr went on to introduce John of the Mountains to her more famous friend, Ralph Waldo Emerson, and to play matchmaker for Muir and his wife Louie. The 30-year correspondence between Jeanne and John helped Muir transform his delightful storytelling skills into defining writings for a new scripture of Nature—a modern bible, or at least a woody gospel, not only to engender national parks but to plant the seeds of a wider and wilder environmental ethic.

Muir died 100 years ago last Christmas Eve (1914) and this

Earth Day weekend marks the 177th year of his birth (April 21, 1838). We are still startled, if not shocked, by some of his radical re-definitions of archaic religious language. Maybe he was being playful. Perhaps he simply liked to jab and joust, tickle and tantalize us with his humor. But his primary purpose seemed always directed to that cry in the wilderness—to clear the dust from our eyes and the fog from our minds; to be converted from blindly using the natural world out of human-centered hubris and ignorance; to repent of our religion (juiceless as it is) that insists we look up and away to better worlds while condemning this beautiful garden planet to hell.

Muir was indeed a voice in the wilderness and his natural gospel (torah, veda, qur'an) echoes forward. Maybe if we sipped a little of that sequoia blood and listened more to the wise teachings of the "master spirit of the tree tops" and her fellow preachers, we might learn to respect the only world we have, sauntering on into the wild forests and mountains before us, with curiosity, wonder and delight, as 21st Century Muirs in an ever-new, wildly interesting world.

25

Heaven, Hope and Humanism

(originally posted on *Secular Chaplain*)

I may have made a mistake today. I took a walk with a gentle young man who used to live on the streets of this town. He knew me back in my Street Chaplaincy years. He has a small, cluttered apartment now, where he spends a lot of time alone. Since I like him and he struggles with some health challenges, I usually try to encourage him. We get together for a walk now and then.

Today we sat on a wobbly bench under a huge oak tree at a local university and talked about life. At one point I told him about my teaching and writing. He was puzzled when I said I consider myself a kind of nature or secular chaplain. Here's how the conversation unfolded:

"That doesn't make sense. A chaplain is grounded in a historic world religion."

"Yes, traditionally, but the word 'chaplain' is now used by people of many faiths and no faiths–remember, I was an 'interfaith' chaplain, and now we have 'Humanist' chaplains. They have those at Stanford, Harvard, Rutgers and other schools now."

"So you don't have a religion, but you're grounded in Humanism or Humanities?"

"Yes, kinda. I'm more a Nature person. Aren't we all grounded in the natural world?"

"I suppose. But 'chaplain' means spiritual, doesn't it?"

"Usually, but now it's used in some new ways. It's really about caring, listening, being with people to help."

He was skeptical, and I welcomed his questions.

"So you don't believe there's a God?"

"No, not anymore. I don't believe in the supernatural...something greater than Nature."

"No other life; no heaven?"

"No. I think this is it. We are 'compost', as Whitman put it. And I think that's wonderful and good enough."

He was quiet for a moment.

I asked, "What do *you* believe?"

My friend looked up at the sun filtering through the trees. He grew pensive.

"I don't know. Isn't it kinda nice to think there's a heaven? I like to think there is. My life has been pretty shitty. I haven't really lived."

This was the moment I wondered if I'd said too much. I took a breath.

"That's very honest. I hear you. I understand. It's good to have hope, and life can be pretty shitty sometimes. There are millions who live with that, and believing gives them hope."

We decided to walk back into town and the conversation drifted away from those things. I asked him to play one of his songs he wrote back when I first met him. I was smiling and singing along. It brought back some good memories, when I was his chaplain. I thanked him, encouraging him to write more music. He smiled and hugged me.

As I left him and walked down the street, I had to ask myself some hard questions:

Are there times when it may be best to keep my disbeliefs to myself? Was I taking my friend's hope away, causing him to doubt the beliefs he holds close, beliefs that help him get through a difficult life?

Usually, I'm ok with stirring up some hard thinking about these things, but when an "issue" or a question hurts another person in some way, maybe it's best to hold it back and simply listen?

I'm not sure if I made a mistake. Maybe you have a thought?

26

Secular in the Sanctuary

(originally posted on *Secular Chaplain*)

So, I went to church today...
Yes, you read that correctly. I attended the family church, to show respect (my father-in-law's ashes rest in the garden there) and to see how the church has changed. Well, I have to say, I saw very little change from years past. Still mostly elderly folks—all good people, I think—and some old-time hymns mixed with old-time prayers. All presented in a "progressive" manner, but mixed with so much traditional baggage I had some difficulty seeing the "progress" (keep in mind I was raised in the church and served as a minister for many years).

Overall I can say I felt welcomed (because family attends) and some of the music was good. I even sang an old hymn "Great Is Thy Faithfulness" that we used to sing in chapel at the Christian college. Personalistic theology, but uplifting melody.

I say I felt welcomed, but I need to clarify that. The words used in song, prayer, scripture and sermon were not quite as welcoming. There was a lot about "Brothers and Sisters in Christ" (what if visitors like me were not Christian?) and sin ("we're all sinners" was supposed to make us all feel better, I guess) and a biblical passage from Genesis about a whole city full of "wickedly" sinful people God (graciously) promises not to nuke because there were a few "righteous" residents. I sat in the pew thinking: "Gee, I guess I'm a wicked sinner here." Almost made me proud...almost.

Another bible passage was read from Luke where The First Christian (Jesus, it's assumed) taught his famous prayer but also said "ask and you shall receive, seek and you shall find, knock and the door will be opened." That was a pop song in my high school youth group. Now, I find it strange and almost cruel. It implies that you'll get what you ask for from your "divine Parent" (Santa?). How many have read that for centuries, asked God for something and NOT received it, sought and NOT found, knocked on God's door and no one was home? I remember being taught: When you don't get what you ask for it means you are either too sinful or "God has something better for you." Nice dance there. In other words, Jesus didn't really mean what he said.

The sermon was pretty good. The woman pastor told some good stories and one actually brought a tear to my eye. The main message seemed to be prayer and mercy, especially God's mercy to us. Here again, all I could think of was: What does that really mean? I think it means we are "lost" without that mercy because a Judge can be merciful to a criminal, or something. It left me wondering: If you replace GOD with PARENT, maybe a parent shows more "mercy" to their child than most of what we hear from God–doesn't it seem that way? At least a parent doesn't demand that their child constantly ask them for things, praise and adore them, then threaten to punish them with everlasting timeout in a very hot room if they don't obey and believe every word they say!

Once again, I think this church is full of good people, and a generally nice message of love and goodness and acceptance is presented. This is true in many congregations I've served and visited. These folks are very welcoming of people of color, LGBTQ folks and others. I think people are simply unaware that their "Good News" isn't really very good to hear, at least for many of us who don't accept the basic assumptions (WE are God's People, there IS a God listening to "God's People," the Bible has authority for today, Church is a meaningful, relevant thing to do in a contemporary, pluralistic city, etc.).

I'll probably go back again. There is almost always something–*something*–to take from the experience of a congregation of believers. Yet. . .I often wonder. . .what might happen if other voices, other minds, were allowed and welcomed to speak up and speak out? What if other faiths, and seculars, were invited to speak, give sermons or be interviewed in church? Why not? Why fear that radical inclusiveness? (This happens in some places –interfaith gatherings, UU fellowships, etc–but not enough, in my way of thinking).

I couldn't help staring out the (minimal) windows during the service to enjoy the green, growing trees and a few notes from a choir of lively birds. Beauty so close by, but unnoticed. Have you ever wondered that "sanctuary" often seems to be just outside so many places we humans call "sanctuary"?

27

The Day I Went to Hell

(a "True" Story)

With a burning desire to speak out and a (very thirsty) tongue-in-cheek...

The following is a "true" story (*feel free to ignore the quotations*).

So many people are writing "true" stories of going to Heaven. Well, I may be the first to tell this incredible, truer than "true" story...

I went to Hell! And came back to tell the world about it (and hopefully write a bestseller and have a blockbuster movie made!).

I might have been dreaming but one mid-afternoon, as a lay on my lawnchair (haven't had one for years, but it appeared and I had to use it) looking up into the sun coming through the trees, a black and white bird landed on the branch above me and something dropped. When I opened my eyes...

I was in HELL.

I didn't know what else to call it. It was just so...hellish. I stood on the edge of a burning lake and looked down at my melted sandals. It was hot, but "hot" can't describe the heat. It was like standing on the surface of the SUN, but since I've never done that–you just have to believe me when

I say it was HOT.

This is a short "true" story, so let me describe what I saw:

All around this lake were people (and a lot of dogs), and thousands, millions, maybe billions, were swimming too. They almost looked like they were having fun, diving in, catching some rays and getting great exercise, but their screams gave it away: this was Suffering Central—the anti-paradise. I couldn't tell if the the howls were louder from the people or the dogs.

Then something truly awful happened. I started to recognize people (and a dog that once bit me). I saw children I used to play with in school; I saw some of my cousins; I saw my dear, sweet grandmother and my cigar-chewing grandfather.

Then, *Oh Hell*, I saw some of my beloved teachers and. . .then the worst: My Parents! This can't be! My parents were good churchgoing people. Among the kindest, most loving people I've ever known. Dad mowed the church lawn every week, gave generously to the offering plate, said grace before *every* meal, and had a very deep faith (I thought!). Mom was my great inspiration! Why were these good folks here in Hell?

Oh, it gets worse!

I waded into the fiery lake (the sand was getting hot ... oddly, the lake fire was slightly cooler), and I was startled to see Neanderthals and African peoples I'd read about in *National Geographic*. There were Vikings and Celts, Goths and Mongols, Romans and Pagans as far as I could see, every Religion was represented (I could tell from the symbols on their bathing suits). I saw endless faces of people of all colors and languages from all lands, screaming out in their own tongues. It was almost beautiful ... a Choir ... almost.

This couldn't be! Suddenly swimming nearby: Socrates, Plato, Aristotle, Emperor Marcus Aurelius, then, George Washington! What!? Then Jefferson, Lincoln, Frederick Douglass, Elizabeth Cady Stanton and John Muir! John Muir??

Ok, I had to *ask* someone what was going on here?

Just at that moment, a white-robed figure glowing brighter than all the fire appeared beside me and put his hand on my shoulder. I recognized him—or maybe it was Her—: it was GOD! Well, I guessed it was God and can't say I'd seen Him or Her before, but I *knew* it must be The One.

A calm voice spoke: "My child. I know you're confused. This is a pretty bad scene. Don't be afraid. You see you're not alone. You are here to suffer with good company. And don't worry, all you see and feel is a part of my divine plan of Love."

I stared at this bright, smiling, strangely chilling face with a skeptical expression.

The voice continued: "I know it must be hard to believe, but everyone you see here deserves to be burned alive–well, actually, burned dead–for the rest of their lives–that is, the rest of their restless death. Sorry, even I get a little confused sometimes about this.

You see, I created this place, what you call HELL, because I love you all so very, very much! I know that's hard to swallow (oh, here, have a scalding cup of tea to sooth your scorching throat–[I think I saw a slight grin]). Everyone you see here, from the beginning of time, will be tortured here in this exquisitely-designed pit of punishment because of one thing:

They just didn't believe in Me. . .the *real* Me. . .the *only* ME that matters. . .the correct Me that the world needs to believe in to be saved from this eternal execution. If they'd only believed in Me–the LORD of LOVE. . . ."

He seemed to get choked up a little at that.

Looking around, I could see something that looked like a tear coming down his face, but it quickly evaporated in the heat.

I couldn't cry. I couldn't speak. This made absolutely no sense, but I knew it would be futile to argue with the Creator of the Universe, especially the Creator of a place so awful and terrible and murderously monstrous.

He continued to try to explain this amazing sight before me. . .but I quietly waded deeper into the lake. He seemed lost in thought and mumbling on about his "abiding love" and "compassionate justice" and "true faith." As the burning waters closed over my head I saw Ben Franklin swimming by with Thomas Paine; Walt Whitman was floating on his back beside Jane Goodall and Carl Sagan, pointing up to what looked like shooting stars and comets on the ceiling of the sooty chamber. I caught a glimpse of a team led by Susan B. Anthony playing a hot game of flaming volleyball with the Planned Parenthood team.

I woke up in my lawnchair. The sun was hot on my face. I was so relieved to breathe the cool air and touch a hand to my head.

I knew it was all "true."

I was REALLY there! Really in HELL! It's REAL!

This is the truest "true" story you will ever hear. And I know exactly what it MEANS! It's now my mission to spread the Word.

Now, listen close.
This may be among the most important messages you *ever* hear! This may be one of the greatest questions you'll *ever* ask!
Are you ready for it?

WHO would make such a place as Hell?

28

Memorials (and Weddings) Without God

Our local interfaith council referred a family to me. They were looking for someone to lead a memorial service for their father who just passed away at 100 years old. They said "Ted," a well-known designer, wasn't really religious but loved nature and considered himself "eco-spiritual." I explained that I am not religious either, that I am also nature-oriented, and I have led many memorials. The family was happy to find someone like me.

Here is what a memorial can be like without God (or supernatural god-talk):

About 20 family and friends gathered in the family home designed by Ted.

I stood with my back to the large window overlooking the sunny yard with green grass, oaks and the hills beyond. Everyone could enjoy the view of Ted's "sanctuary."

We took some deep breaths as I gently explained we were there to "celebrate one life: Ted's life...and LIFE itself–our lives." I said that the day was good because life was good, even with the grief that shouldn't be denied or avoided–it was ok to cry.

I said we throw too many words at the mysteries of life, especially death, when we really don't know what to say. This was one reason the memorial was brief. They could all tell more stories over the meal later.

I asked the circle to close their eyes and whisper the name they called Ted. Then to open their eyes and speak that name (dad, grandpa, etc) looking at others. A sweet moment.

I quoted a line from Ted where he spoke of his drawing board. We smiled to consider Life's drawing boards. I spoke of his "eco-spirituality." Since he was an architectural designer I said "eco" was an ancient word for "house or home." People were pleasantly surprised by that.

I quoted a line from John Muir (who died about the time Ted was born 100 years ago). Muir spoke of nature being a part and parent of us and that Beauty was the best word for God. People really seemed to like that.

I invited anyone to say a few words or tell a story (why call it "eulogies"?). This was of course the heart of our time together. Many laughs, smiles and tears.

I encouraged everyone to hold on to the special name they called Ted, and to hold on to the stories and lessons of his life. "You will learn from him for a very long time...maybe 100 years!"

We ended with my reading the last lines of Walt Whitman's "Song of Myself," with the famous line, "I sound my barbaric yawp over the roofs of the world" and "I stop somewhere waiting for you." Many smiles at the reference to homes and roofs–Ted's drawing board.

They played a piece of music Ted enjoyed. That brought many to tears.

Everyone thanked me very much afterward with handshakes and hugs. The daughter gave me a bag of fresh vegetables from the garden. The son handed me a check for more than I asked for. There was great appreciation.

A joyful, secular memorial without religion. We need to actively offer these as "live options" for families. No Gods...but lots of Good.

But let me also say, no doubt there were people of faith in the room. Among the family and friends there were surely a few who were believers. They were welcome. They could have offered a brief scripture or prayer or mention of God. But none did that. They were respecting the wishes of Ted and his widow Beth to have a non-religious ceremony.

This is the great gift of Secular Ceremonies. They are inclusive in a way religious ceremonies can never be. The moment you call upon One God from One Tradition, you exclude everyone else. No matter how much a leader intends to be inclusive, that can't really be possible in these deeply meaningful and emotional times. And most importantly: families are usually pretty diverse in beliefs, so why not simply guide them through a close experience of death by "celebrating life" allowing each one to handle their grief with whatever beliefs they choose? As with *marriage ceremonies*, why inject sectarian religious beliefs into the celebration (also a Celebration of Life!).

God is not necessary to celebrate the Good. Religion is simply not necessary to create relevant, meaningful gatherings.

This is why I think we need more Secular Ceremonies to truly honor the diversity of our contemporary communities. I have seen for myself how very much appreciated this approach can be.

Near the end of the gathering, Ted's widow Beth told us how Ted would sometimes look up at the trees and the hills beyond and say, "That's my prayer and I know it will be answered." A very natural expression of his hopes, rooted to the land where he lived, and the family he loved.

Thank you for the gift of your life, Ted.

. . .

Secular people love celebrations of Life in any form. I have led countless memorials over the years, mostly for poor people who had no family to remember them or "celebrate their lives." It is actually a great honor and privilege to lead these celebrations, especially for people outside religious communities.

This is why I also enjoy celebrating *weddings* as a Humanist Celebrant. Working with couples to craft a ceremony that fits them can be a lot of fun. I first led a wedding by a backyard swimming pool in Marin County, California all the way back in 1987 (see photos from a variety of celebrations on my *Friendly Freethinker* website). Over the years I was honored to share a number of these joyful moments with my friend, rabbi Jerry Winston. I think the image of a rabbi and minister presiding at such occasions left an indelible picture for many couples and families. On another occasion I joined a Hindu priest to conduct an elaborate ceremony.

Probably the ultimate for me was in 2009 when my wife Carol and I were thrilled to have four of our clergy friends leading our own wedding celebration. Some friends and family were stunned to see a Christian minister, Buddhist priest, Jewish rabbi and Wiccan witch presiding. Each one a colleague, and all women! No one will forget that day, least of all us.

Couples have written to me after their weddings to express their deep gratitude. One happy couple wrote: *"Weddings are about you, and your significant other. They're a celebration of love, and commitment, and Chris always made sure to keep the focus on that, and honestly, gave a flawless performance as our officiant. He understood our goals and desires, and on top of that, is an awesome person to have a beer with."*

I quote this not to show how wonderful I am but to stress that this non-religious couple (the groom was a brewer, the bride a teacher) were looking for someone to create and lead their secular wedding ceremony in a meaningful way. This is what a freethinking celebrant can do for countless couples who simply wish to celebrate their love in a "god-free" or at least faith-free environment.

There is a great need for secular leaders to step into the widening gap between the religious and non-religious, where many clergy fear to tread (and frankly aren't trained for it). It's very satisfying to know you have performed an important service for people during a critical transition in their lives, whether a baby naming, wedding, memorial or brand new innovative event.

29

Farkhunda: Martyr for Us All

(from *The Natural Bible* blog)

With more recent tragic events in Afghanistan, I was taken back to 2015, and an intensely disturbing story in *The New York Times* that not only caught my attention, but haunted me for days (NYT, Dec. 27, 2015). Deeply troubling, it was also inspiring. Inspiring can mean "taking a deep breath" to reflect and learn.

A mentally ill woman is accused of burning pages of the Qur'an ... so, of course, she's brutally killed by a mob.

Her name was **Farkhunda**. It happened at a shrine. She seemed to be very religious while making others feel uncomfortable in their devotion. It was acceptable to pay their respects at a shrine like this, she instructed visitors, but it was not an appropriate place to worship. "Don't come here to pray," she shouted, according to a certain Mr. Mohammad. "God won't accept your prayers here."

In ancient times, she may have been called a Prophet (they were often thought of as "crazy people," with their bizarre words and antics–just read Ezekiel...or any biblical babbler who pointed their dirty finger at the self-righteous).

One of the oddest and craziest things about Religion throughout its history is the defense and protection of holy books (and sanctuaries, and theologies) over human persons. People will kill the innocent to protect a book that instructs not to kill the innocent. People will be enraged to hate, over a book that supposedly teaches love. People will burn someone with even a suspicion they have burned a page of "holy words."

Madness. Yet, *She* is the madwoman!

When I was a street chaplain, in one of the wealthiest counties in America, I led something like 100 memorial services for people who died without housing. . .in a county full of "holy places"—churches, synagogues, mosques, temples. Popular stores carried lots of bibles, torahs, qur'ans, sutras, and hundreds of other "spiritual books" by any guru and new age "teacher" you can name—and many you can't.

Yet, people die on the streets. Sometimes right outside the heavy, locked stained glass doors of the Houses of God—Mansions for the Masses. Many of the ones who die were (and are) as mentally ill as **Farkhunda**. Do we kill them? Not directly. Do we accuse them, make them criminals, make it very hard to find shelter and a place to call home, make them outcasts who are usually unwelcomed in the pure places for piety? Yes.

Then, often, the weakest die. Many are veterans, many are women, many are sick or mentally wounded. Year after year we see them die. Or, we don't see them. We don't want to.

Does a brutal, inhumane mob of righteous defenders (or bored youth) stone and burn them? Not here. Not yet. We may silence them in other, cleaner, more "acceptable" ways. We still "shoot our wounded," but our weapons are ignorance, prejudice, hypocrisy and, perhaps most brutal, choosing not to see, or care.

And, as I see it, often the most deadly weapons are our ancient holy books that stir emotions and distract attention up and away to imagined heavens in the sky, seeking personal acceptance of righteousness and salvation, while condemning the world and its walking wounded to hell. I fault Liberals and Progressives as much as Conservatives for this. Turning a blind eye is not only a Right Wing malady.

Is all the blame on believers? Of course not. Our political leaders often have narrow vision with even narrower thinking. And the self-righteous "moral leaders," who preach "love and justice"? Where are they?

Are there some who speak out, who stand up, who stand beside those who are vulnerable. Thankfully, yes. Like the worried hatmaker who observed with alarm what they did to **Farkhunda**, who watched the mob from his shop, and condemned the attack as inhuman.

"What they did is brutal and completely against Islam," said the hatmaker, Sayed Habib Saadat. A hatmaker.

Kabul. A world away. Yet, perhaps, not really so far.

Farkhunda.
Remember her.
. . .

My story of the terrible killing of Farkhunda in Kabul had over 1300 views on my blog. As one whose "spiritual ancestors" (heretics) were burned for their beliefs or non-beliefs ... I will never stand by and watch a person put down or raised up to disrespect, harass, injure or murder in the Name of a Religion or the Name of a God.

If your "holy book" is more sacred, holy, revered than a Human Life, more respected than Reason, than Freedom ... you are dangerous and should expect to be confronted by the force of Truth and True Justice.

I don't condone the burning of holy books. But if the choice is to burn pages or people ... a freethinking person will leave their books and Live the Words.

Think about it: Did any of the so-called Great Spiritual Teachers (Moses, Jesus, Muhammad, Buddha, Confucius...) carry a holy book around or hand out copies? *Did they ever say Scriptures were more Sacred than a Human Being?* Of course not. They were writing the holy books with their lives.

Remember Farkhunda.
Maybe burning her was the real desecration of a living holy book.
Remember Farkhunda.
(and Hypatia, Narendra Dabholkar, Avijit Roy, the staff of Charlie Hebdo, and all others across the world who have suffered, and continue to suffer, for Free Speech, Free-thought and Human Rights)

Note: see *Humanists International* for the current status of freethinkers being persecuted or prosecuted around the world.

30

The Bible of Nature
(Secular Scripture)

"Miles and miles of tree scripture along the sky, a bible that will one day be read! The beauty of its letters and sentences have burned me like fire through all these Sierra seasons."
~John Muir, Letter to Jeanne Carr (September, 1874)

Those of us who have chosen to wander "off trail" to find or make our own paths in non-supernatural wilds, sometimes wonder if there are any maps left for the adventure forward. When we're not busy sketching our own maps, we may stop to realize we are living in the great map...and, there are no maps.

In *Nature's God*, Matthew Stewart tells us the only book in the (Connecticut) village where Revolutionary War hero Ethan Allen grew up, was the Bible. That certainly wasn't unusual in rural settlements in the New World or Old. Naturalist John Muir, as a young boy, had to sneak books to read by candlelight in the family's farmhouse basement in Wisconsin because his self-styled Scottish preacher father was a Bible-only believer. Muir's freethinking (like his free-climbing in the mountains) caused him to leave the Bible far back on the trail. He had it memorized anyway, as his Alaska missionary friend, Samuel Hall Young, wrote in 1915: "I had my printed Bible with me, and he had his in his head--the result of a Scotch father's discipline" (*Alaska Days with John Muir*).

For Ethan Allen, as for Muir, there was one Good Book in their brain, but the "Bible of Nature" became a much more alive and accessible text for ethical, spiritual guidance as well as philosophical and scientific knowledge, and even political action. This unbound book was not only wide open and fascinating but actually taught itself, if a student was paying attention. As Allen--author of his own "bible," *Oracles of Reason* (1784)--put it, anyone with sense can learn everything worth knowing from "the air we breathe in, the light of the sun, the waters of the murmuring hills," in the "rainy and fair seasons, monsoons and refreshing breezes, feed time and harvest, day and night" (Stewart, p. 47). A bit later, the seeds of this new natural gospel were harvested in Thomas Paine's dual revolutions in government and religion, throwing out the old and planting the new.

Entering the Alaskan frontier, Muir was amused when the missionaries he was sailing with forgot their missions and bibles as the magnificent mountain ranges came into view. "The earnest, childish wonderment with which this glorious page of Nature's Bible was contemplated was delightful to see" (*Travels in Alaska*, 1915). The young naturalist couldn't wait to leap into his "mountains of God." But what did Muir mean by this "God"? In a journal entry scribbled down in June 1875, he wrote this piece of heresy: "No synonym for God is so perfect as Beauty.... All is Beauty!"

Muir's friend, John Burroughs, developed these infidel insights in an essay called "The Gospel of Nature" (see *Time and Change*, 1912). Burroughs, like Muir, was raised in a religious family and once considered the ministry. The heretic spirit was too strong in him though and something greater than God was calling him. "Except ye become in a measure as little children, ye cannot enter the kingdom of Nature." As Burroughs let go of the old religion, a new and improved version, a new translation, was appearing.

"The forms and creeds of religion change, but the sentiment of religion—the wonder and reverence and love we feel in the presence of the inscrutable universe—persists." He knew the language of faith well, and completely reshaped it for our age.

Each of these naturalistic thinkers was like a schoolchild hearing the bell and running out the doors to a much more interesting and exciting School that welcomed their delightful curiosity. Muir's famous line when he left the University of Wisconsin echoes this anticipation: "I was only leaving one University for another. . .the University of the Wilderness" (*My Boyhood and Youth*, 1912). And, he was leaving one Church for another; one Bible for another; one worldview for another. What a liberating feeling! What a sense of graduation!

Could it be that this new, wild Bible--this scripture spread out over the untamed landscapes--is no bible or scripture at all? Could it be that this "holy book," with no origin outside our universe, is such an amazing, living record of our wildness in this wilderness of space that everything is holy and nothing at all is "holy"?

The incredible beauty of the world and the cosmos makes super-natural faith fade like the fog in the sun. The grass withers, the flower fades, faith dies, but the word of Nature lives on.

If there is a relevant "ministry" and a "calling" left to hear, left to teach if not to preach, maybe it's quite literally in the "call of the wild," the Gospel of Beauty heralded by our Nature Prophets who forever point us toward what Emerson identified as "the most ancient religion."

After a walk through a redwood forest today, I stood quietly by a late summer stream. It was a gentle reminder that all those years in the Church, all the years of biblical study and ministry, all the books and "spiritual lessons" taught me no more than this day in the woods. This is the only scripture I need. The only good news to teach and never preach. The only "spirituality" that remains. All is Beauty; all is secular. This is the Greatest Bible there is, with letters and sentences that burn like fire, wherever the paths may lead.

31

Last Supper for the Dying Church

A liberally progressive church in San Francisco invited me to speak as a representative of "naturalistic freethinkers." Since I was writing and teaching about "wild spirituality," this was...natural for me (note: I don't teach that any longer).

When I arrived I was warmly welcomed by the tattooed music director, a young "neighborhood chaplain" sipping a beer (from the memorial celebration just before the service), and the smiling pastor in her long white robe. They made sure I found a cup of Earl Grey and had a seat in the circle by the pastor.

We sang some lively hymns accompanied by a beautiful guitar and peppy piano.

I spoke on "Nature and Wonder: Secular Spirituality," quoting Carl Sagan, John Burroughs and Frances Wright. A really delightful time for questions showed that people were quite curious about non-believing, freethinking, issues of truth and raising children to think for themselves by choosing from alternatives. They laughed that I prefer not to use "the A-word" and nodded when I explained I choose not to live my life identified with negativity...that I am not anti-religious, anti-believer.

And then came the Body and the Blood, Eucharist, Communion, the Last Supper.

I asked the pastor before the service how they handled people who chose not to take the "elements." She good-naturedly said that was fine and that not everyone in the congregation went up to receive Communion.

It *was* fine. No pressure. No accusing glances. The familiar "Invitation to the Table" was spoken, but not with a tone of false piety or somber sappy sweetness. Funny thing is, I almost went forward! They were so welcoming and inclusive and loose about it. I know I would not have been judged for not believing the bread was anything but bread and the wine was anything but wine. But, I chose to sit and smile and wait for the end.

As a former Christian minister, I've led many communion services over the years. As an Interfaith chaplain I led a whole lot of "community meals" that were wildly inclusive, among people of many faiths and who-knows-what-they-believe. Now, as a non-believer among believers, I reflected on the Non-Supernatural meaning of this ritual. I thought how diverse people sharing a "meal" could, if they really wanted to, put aside differences of opinion and simply enjoy being together. Maybe it would lead to working together, regardless of faith or no faith. Sure, mention Jesus, but let go of all the artificial add-ons and theo-mythology!

I suppose this experience renewed my hope in small circles of human beings, people who have the good intention to be good and do good in their neighborhood, their world. Yes, I would do away with the distracting and divisive God-language, but even with a little of that, there is potential for "community" to grow, inch by inch, row by row.

Postscript: One person told me privately that the church was "dying." They are attempting to create a community center, while based in their religious tradition. I cautiously supported that idea, suggesting they consider letting go of some of the religious icons so more people would feel they are entering a safe space where they won't be Faithenized.

I could almost imagine these small communities might welcome more of us who are former Insiders, to help in the transition of the dying church into...Something Better!

Maybe, just maybe, *Freethinkers could Save the Church* (from itself)!

32

Damn My Secular Soul

(the wrestling match for reason, God, opinions...)

The Secular/Spiritual merry-go-round can be a dizzying carousel sometimes. Online comment may progress to conversation with potential for dialogue and meaningful debate. Or not.

Engaging believers *can* be productive and interesting. And sometimes the opposite. There's just no telling. The following exchange between chaplains may sound familiar to those who wander out on the minefield of blog commenters...

I recently came across a priest who refers to himself as a chaplain. He posted an alarmist article about the U.S. Air Force cracking down on a chaplain in Alaska who was posting sermons attacking atheists. The priest was obviously agitated about this "censorship" and the "religious freedom" under attack (notice how quickly this becomes an attack on *Christians*, when the problem began as Christians attacking *atheists*).

So, being who I am, I commented. Here's my first one:

"In nearly every instance of "an attack on religious freedom" it is conservative Christians crying out they are persecuted when there is no evidence of this. Those who want Christians to continue to dominate chaplaincy seem to have no memory of "do unto others," which remains the most difficult teaching

for Christians to actually follow. If the military of our secular nation has to have Chaplains (and I'm not convinced we need them) there has to be accommodation to all faith and ethical traditions. This post is yet another alarm bell for special privileges. It sounds rather tinny."

This seemed to set the priest off. Our back and forth began with him telling me he's a retired British Intelligence officer (not sure if this was supposed to intimidate me?) and the whole secular culture has lost the "Judeo-Christian doctrine and ethic."

I scribbled back:

"Ok, sir, yet the article is on the American military and, in my opinion, the violation of the establishment of religion clause in our constitution. Hard to see your point regarding the "loss" of any Christian influence (dominance) in our cultures, though the point could be made that there is a decline in some ethics when any religion takes power and arrogantly dominates. Why wouldn't Christians support chaplains of all ethical groups if they really care about all personnel?"

I'll spare you the details of his life, but he isn't happy with this "secular" stuff:

"Speaking for myself, a "secular" chaplain is an oxymoron, a real opposite! But in this time of both modernity & postmodernity, I am certainly not surprised!"

When he started quoting "born again" passages, I was irritated and tried some good old sarcasm:

"Well, sir, I'm not sure much discussion can come from our perspectives here, but you may be correct in suggesting I'm both an oxy and a moron (smiling here). Welcome to the U.S.. I

apologize for our godless constitution and secular nation built on freedom of religion (free to choose a religion, or not). Sorry we were never or will never be a Christian country. I often wonder, what is the goal of those who preach for a "return to Judeo-Christian" things? "Jesusland" USA only exists in some peoples' fantasy world.

By the way, my almost 30 years as a chaplain in one form or another, faith and no faith, taught me one main thing: no one owns or controls the truth, and, truth is, people are in need of much more than preaching (and quoting holy books simply doesn't help). I wish you well."

Well, the preacher-priest-chaplain wasn't finished, and he obviously didn't appreciate the sarcasm.

"Funny Chris, and I never said the American Constitution was "godless" and "secular", your words and conclusion, not mine."

He went on about being a "Biblicist" (bible worshipper?) and a "neo-Calvinist" so I knew I was done (well done, burned to a crisp, in Calvinistic Hell). He mentioned my eternal soul, so I finally concluded (duh) it was time to turn down the volume and sign off.

"I guess I asked for the preaching, by commenting here. As a former seminary-trained minister and a student of the bible for many years, I have to say it sounds quite hollow to have it pushed back in my face. But, it's your blog, so expected.

Beyond that, one final comment: in your passion to convert the world to your opinion you might keep in mind that it is often secular people like me (and like Jefferson, Franklin, Paine and other freethinkers) who most protect your right to believe as you wish and speak freely. This is the strength of a secular state where religious freedom is vigorously supported by a

Constitution and Bill of Rights based on reason and diversity rather than on one dominant theological opinion. Yes, a clergyman signed the declaration, alongside Deists and Freethinkers. Independent minds working together. Quite impressive. I wish you well."

After my "sign off," I went back to visit and found that he had left 3 more comments for me beginning with:

"Yes, this is a blog, and a religious blog mate, and not really a secular place, i.e. modernity and postmodernity!"

And, he was a vet who fought for "God and Country" and ... Great.

Well, gosh, and damn my secular soul too.

Was I asking for this? Did I bait him? A little. But what was the purpose of his post and responses to me? To preach. To go after nonbelievers in the service of their country. To quote the bible and show me his profound faith and pietistic patriotism (implying all along that I could not possibly have ethics or be patriotic, and my soul is lost, somewhere!).

So, I suppose this little "conversation" can be taken as a caution, a warning. We choose our fights over these emotionally charged things. Or, we simply choose not to fight but to seek constructive dialogue. For some of us, we can quickly see when that's not going to be possible.

Have you had similar exchanges with preachers and believers? When did you know enough was enough?

33

The New Secular

(hint: it's really the old)

Saeculum: the present world.

As Thoreau said shortly before he died in 1862: "one world at a time." Those who feel we are "at home in the universe" already, have no driving desire to be somewhere else, somewhere better, more beautiful, more blessed. We are, by Nature, naturally secular—of this world.

The *Book of James* in the Christian scriptures instructs believers not to be "stained by the world." Paul was constantly warning the faithful not to give in to "the flesh"–the impurity of the physical, material existence. *The First Letter of John*, as much as it claims that God is Love, says "Do not love the world or the things in the world," and "We know that we are God's children, and that the whole world lies under the power of the evil one." In the *Gospel of John*, Jesus shows his humility (?) before "The Jews" by stating, "You are from below, I am from above; you are of this world, I am not of this world" (8:23).

Apocalyptic dreaming is completely otherworldly and therefore naturally (read: un-naturally) focuses on the imperfection of this world; believers can't wait to get to "the other side" "up there" beyond. As a youthful evangelical and charismatic I sang, in an almost ecstatic trance with my friends, "Heaven is a wonderful place...I want to see my

Savior's face," "I've got a home in gloryland ... away beyond the blue!" and many other songs of longing for another world. The dream of heaven (really the "sky" for ancient people) was of no concern for the Hebrews who seem to have acquiesced to "the grave" as the end of life–then one's offspring carry on the family name and memory; one's children (or creative work and ideas) are the only eternal life.

"Sacred" has been presented, throughout religious history, as the opposite of "Secular." Anything not of "this world" is superior and holy, set apart in the realm or reign of God. This universal schizophrenia has fractured and decimated whole nations and entire cultures leading to massive atrocities, staggering wars and appalling violence. Though Hitler, Stalin and Mao are often held up by the religious as the best evidence for the moral degradation of atheism, could any of these have had the wide destructive impact if religion was not involved or complicit? And let's be honest, faith *was* involved in those dictatorships, so we have to ask why more rational religious believers weren't living their faith?" (would the Taliban, Trumpublicans or other Faith Fascists be so powerful if not for weak religious resistance?). It begs the question, Where is the sacred at all? In another world beyond the clouds? In "holy" bread, wine, grapejuice or water touched by "holy hands"? Under the priestly robes or in the holy of holies?

What makes a "sanctuary" a sacred place and not "worldly?" What if the whole universe is sanctuary, in the sense of Good, Beautiful and "Blessed?" Some "progressives" might tend to agree, until we remind them that it is WE who bless, WE who deem it sanctuary and have to live with that. And there remains the nasty problem of the secular/sacred, flesh/spiritual divide that no faith can sidestep for long.

Isn't this all death to the intellect? Isn't it silly and foolish? Of course. Dividing the Universe into the Up There and the Down Here, which pretty much every religion teaches, ends rational discussion, constructive cooperation and certainly decisive environmental action. In recent days Evangelical voices are calling their flocks to be "good stewards" of the environment, that is, "God's Creation." Fine, to a point. But how many religious folks are willing to work beside non-religious women and men to take care of the earth, the home we all share? There will always be a limit to how much the Sacred/Secular dichotomy can be pushed. In a two-story universe (or three if you count God's torture chamber) this secular world will always and forever be in the dark and damned basement, with the sacred first story the true dwelling of the sacred and divine and those who serve the "higher" way, the un-secular chosen.

Doesn't a more "secular" understanding and worldview make better sense for today? Does the fact that there is no first floor, no basement, no house at all, frighten us? It is not necessary to be afraid. We all live in a house with one room, as Muir reminded us. Maybe it's all sacred or all secular, but what does it matter? The cosmos is as it is no matter what we call it. If it helps a person to think of it all as sacred, fine. As long as there is no greater value placed on an invented reality called "super-natural," on something "higher." We do not live in the Twilight Zone or the Outer Limits, though fiction that is based on Science and Art can be stimulating and entertaining. But we are no longer entertained by faith that judges the present world, the secular, as deficient or "profane" (another destructive archaic expression). It is not entertainment to be devalued as "only flesh," "only human," "of the world."

It seems probable that Life does indeed go on forever; death is never the end. Atoms and molecules continue. We are secular immortals. We are of the humus, humbly of earth, dirt-Human. And perhaps we will one day soon live up to our name, *Homo Sapiens*: genus of the wise, in this present, secular age.

Secular Holidays

When the spring season rolls around again, once more we have Easter, and Passover, and countless other religious holidays around the spinning world of spirituality. Millions of Hindus recently washed their sins away in the rivers of India. Pagans celebrate the Goddess and the life (and execution) of the ancient freethinker Hypatia of Alexandria. Bahai's and Zoroastrians have their special days. Catholics have a new Pope and Buddhists have the same old Dalai Lama (I can see him smiling).

Some of us "only" celebrate Spring. We only welcome a new season––the *Green Season* decorated with new buds and birds and a bit of rain. Our only rituals are walks by the streams, lakes or bays, or deep breaths in the wild woods, listening for the choirs of hawks and frogs, turkeys and coyotes. We only delight in the verdant vivaciousness of fresh living things–and we feel a part of that freshness. We only honor the incredible (beyond belief) beauty of the amazing "homeworld" we share with all creatures small and great, alongside those with super-natural faith and those who simply, joyfully, see the natural world as good and super enough just as it is.

Most of us who left "the faith" (or who never had it) aren't anti-religious or anti-god. Who has the time or energy for being against things all the time? No, most of us who identify as "other" or "unaffiliated" or maybe as agnostic, humanist or freethinker, aren't interested in dividing the world into insiders and outsiders (that's been done for us, sad to say, often by religion). No, we have family and friends, colleagues and companions who are members of churches and synagogues, mosques and temples. We may even attend with them now and then. They look to God; we look to Good, and we mostly get along. We seem to find a way to live and work side by side rather peaceably.

Maybe we all need a holiday. Dare I say it, perhaps a holiday, at least now and then, from religion, faith and god. Sorry. Don't mean to offend. Marin (my home for many years before transplanting to North Carolina) is full of the faithful and the unfaithful...I mean, non-believers. Many of us were, and are, the *heretics*; the *infidels*. In the land of fast-food faith, where you can channel or chant, pray or praise, sing or sit in silence, to whomever or whatever you call divine, we are the outsiders, those irritating folk who "believe" that believing isn't everything, that distractions of theology and holy books sometimes need to be set aside. Those distractions can be dangerous, if we leave reason and reasonable discourse outside of public meetings and community issues that affect us all, believing or not.

No matter what some bestsellers are telling us, no one can say whether there really is another world out there. *What we can say though is that this present ("secular") world exists, and here we are. Now, what do we do? This is the ethical question, faith or no faith.* Truth is, we live in the midst of such immense beauty that some reverent appreciation couldn't hurt; some daily delight in the endlessly fascinating wonder of it all might actually help. Could we just celebrate that?

A non-believer's holiday isn't about disrespecting anyone's religion or destroying someone's faith. This isn't about closing all the holy places and shoving all sacred objects into a closet. We're only searching for a better way to piece together human community where everyone is a valued, contributing member.

Believe it, or not, *every day is a non-believer's holiday*. But it's not about belief or non-belief. That's the point.

AFTERWORD

Streaming

Sheltered in the old cabin high in the mountains for another short winter's week, my brother and I snowshoed around the mossy boulders and glacier-ground cairns of stone, touched the massive bark arms of time-worn trees and crisscrossed icy burns and rivers. We were delightfully dowsed in sun, soil, snow and stream.

After putting my hand in the deep-chilled mountain waters a few times, hearing and feeling the power of snow-swirling winds, standing under the night-show of sprinkled stars, I paused for the Great Gospel of the Mountains, thinking:

All is a Stream. All of it.

All that. All this. All of us.

Me. You. Everyone. Everything.

Streams of clouds drop streams of rain and snow blown by streams of wind and strike the land to become streams of water moving, bubbling down and down through forest and canyon, falling in streaming light.

Streams of cells and sap and fiber root and crown the streams of bark-clothed streaming beings we call trees.

Streams of birds and insects, fish and invisibles circle and cycle in endless movement.

Streams of air are drawn into our cave-like openings to stream along the branches of lungs to energize the streams of blood that we streamdwellers call Life and Living.

We do dwell in streams. We are streams. Living Rivers in a Universal River.

One stream filled with endless streams.

Nature is Stream.

. . .

The Silent Skipping-Stone

We are
sauntering upon a soggy stone
an infinitesimal rock spinning through space
As if. . .someone threw us, skipping across
the dark ocean of the milky galaxy
It makes sense—
We so desperately long for, search for, assurance, to be comforted,
to be told we are important—to someone
that we are thought of, cared for
that we are watched over and protected
until welcomed "home"—somewhere (where the skipping stops and sinks).
Our spinning, skipping stone
is ours alone
alone
alone together
swirling on our only home—
the only one we think we know.
Skipping.
As if. . .someone dropped a fecund seed

on a massive marble of muck
and forests and meadows and plains sprouted with virescence.
Skipping.
As if...someone sparked a cell to *life*—what's that?—and it evolved into organisms pregnant with animals including us.
Skipping.
As if...WHY do we do this to ourselves!
WHY do we speculate and postulate and gravitate to
As if's?
Don't our eyes tell us, our senses sensitize us, to common sense?
Why skip our reason?
We wonder, we imagine, we dream, we hope.
And after thousands of years
distracted by our wandering imagination,
the Rock still spins.
We travel without going anywhere (at least anywhere that matters to us—we don't perceive it anyway; we can't conceive of it anyway!).
We're going nowhere...but 600 million miles—
year after year after century after century...
lifetimes of lifetimes.
Skipping. Sauntering.
A long long way. Standing still at 67,000 miles per hour.
Spinning, rotating at 1000 miles per hour
(and what's an hour? Does time matter?)
Do you matter?
Do we matter?
What does it matter?
As a matter-of-fact:
We're skipping, sauntering through space, on

CHRIS HIGHLAND

Our stone.

ABOUT THE AUTHOR

Chris Highland was born and raised near Seattle, then lived in the San Francisco Bay Area for over three decades. He has degrees from Seattle Pacific University and San Francisco Theological Seminary. He was an interfaith chaplain and Presbyterian minister for many years. He has been a special education instructor in a private school and the director of a county emergency shelter. For six years he was the manager of two cooperative homes for independent seniors.

Chris has taught courses in congregations and been an instructor at Dominican University of California, Cherry Hill Seminary, College of Marin and Blue Ridge Community College. He currently teaches courses on Freethought at the Reuter Center on the campus of the University of North Carolina, Asheville. He writes the weekly "Highland Views" column for the *Asheville Citizen-Times*.

His numerous books include:
From Faith to Freethought
Simply Secular
Nature is Enough
Friendly Freethinker
Broken Bridges
A Freethinker's Gospel
Birds, Beetles, Bears and Beliefs
Was Jesus a Humanist?
The Message on the Mountain
Meditations of John Muir
My Address is a River

Chris is married to Carol Hovis, a Presbyterian minister, counselor and teacher. They live in the Blue Ridge Mountains in Asheville, North Carolina.

For more information:

Friendly Freethinker (www.chighland.com)

To contact Chris: chris.highland@gmail.com

Made in the USA
Middletown, DE
24 March 2024